Bible Studies for Children

Genesis

© 2013 Nazarene Publishing House
ISBN 978-1-56344-759-4

Editor for US English version: William A. Rolfe
Executive Editor for Global English: Allison L. G. Southerland
Managing Editor for non-English versions: Allison L. G. Southerland
Editorial Committee: Dan Harris, Jenni Monteblanco, Nate Owens, Shelby Oxner, Beula Postlewait, Linda Stargel, Scott Stargel
Cover Art: "The Birth of Adam" by Greg White
Director of Sunday School and Discipleship Ministries International: Woodie J. Stevens

Published by
KidzFirst Publications
17001 Prairie Star Parkway
Lenexa, KS 66220 (USA)

This edition published by arrangement with Nazarene Publishing House, Kansas City, Missouri USA

The first Children's Bible Quiz, created by Rev. William (Bill) Young, was introduced with three demonstration teams from the Kansas City District - Kansas City First, Kansas City St. Paul's, and Overland Park - at the 1968 General Nazarene Young People's Society Convention in Kansas City, Missouri (USA).

CONTENTS

WELCOME!

Welcome to *Bible Studies for Children: Genesis!* In this collection of biblical studies, the children will learn about God's holiness and his faithfulness to his people, even when they make a bad choice.

Bible Studies for Children: Genesis is one of six books in the *Bible Studies for Children* series. These studies help children to gain an understanding of biblical chronology and the meaning of biblical events. As the children learn about the lives of the people in these studies, they discover God's love for all people and their place in his plan. God sometimes uses miracles to achieve his purposes. He often works through people to accomplish what he wants to do.

The philosophy of *Bible Studies for Children* is to help the children to understand what the Bible says, to learn how God helped the people, and to know God through a relationship with him. This includes biblical study, biblical memorization, and application of biblical teachings in real life situations.

Bible Studies for Children uses the *New International Version* of the Bible.

BOOKS

The following is a short description of the books in this series and the way that they interact with each other.

Genesis provides the foundation. This book tells how God created the world from nothing, formed a man and a woman, and created a beautiful garden for their home. These people sinned, and they experienced the consequences for their sin. Genesis introduces the plan of God to reconcile the broken relationship between God and the people. It introduces Adam, Eve, Noah, Abraham, Isaac, and Jacob. God made a covenant with Abraham and renewed that covenant with Isaac and Jacob. Genesis ends with the story of Joseph who saves civilization from famine. The famine compels the people of God to move to Egypt.

Exodus tells how God continued to keep his promise to Abraham. God rescued the Israelites from slavery in Egypt. The Lord chose Moses to guide the Israelites. The Lord set up his kingship over the Israelites. He led and ruled the Israelites through the establishment of the priesthood and the Tabernacle, the Ten Commandments and other laws, and the prophets and the judges. At the end of Exodus, only a part of the covenant of the Lord with Abraham is complete.

Joshua/Judges/Ruth tells how God completed his covenant to Abraham that began in Genesis. The Israelites conquered and settled into the land that God promised to Abraham. The prophets, the priests, the Law, and the worship rituals declared that God was the Lord and the King of the Israelites. The 12 tribes of Israel settled into the Promised Land.

This book emphasizes these judges: Deborah, Gideon, and Samson.

In **1 and 2 Samuel**, the Israelites wanted a king because the other nations had a king. These studies tell about Samuel, Saul, and David. Jerusalem became the centre of the combined nation of Israel. This study shows how the people react differently when someone confronted them with their sins. While Saul blamed others or made excuses, David admitted his sin, and he asked God for forgiveness.

Matthew is the focal point of the entire series. It focuses on the birth, the life, and the ministry of Jesus. All the previous books in the series pointed to Jesus as the Son of God and the Messiah. Jesus ushered in a new era. The children learn about this new era in several events: the teachings of Jesus, his death, his resurrection, and the mentoring of his disciples. Through Jesus, God provided a new way for the people to have a relationship with him.

At the beginning of **Acts**, Jesus ascended to heaven, and God sent the Holy Spirit to help the Church. The good news of salvation through Jesus Christ spread to many parts of the world. The believers preached the gospel to the Gentiles, and missionary work began. The message of the love of God transformed both the Jews and the Gentiles. There is a direct connection between the evangelism efforts of Paul and Peter to the lives of the people today.

CYCLE

The following cycle of using this series is specifically for those who participate in the optional quizzing aspect of the *Bible Studies for Children*. You will find more information about this in the section called "Children's Bible Quizzing" on page 112.

Genesis (2013-2014)
Exodus (2014-2015)
Joshua/Judges/Ruth (2015-2016)
1 & 2 Samuel (2016-2017)*
Matthew (2017-2018)
Acts (2018-2019)
Indicates a World Quiz Year

SCHEDULE

Each book in the series has twenty studies. Allow one to two hours of class time. The following schedule is a suggestion for each study.

15 minutes for the **Activity**
30 minutes for the **Biblical Lesson**
15 minutes for the **Memory Verse**
30 minutes for the **Additional Activities** (optional)
30 minutes for the **Quizzing Practice** (optional)

TEACHERS PREPARATION

Thorough preparation of each study is important. The children are more attentive and gain better understanding of the study if you prepare it well and present it well. **Bold text** in each study indicates suggested words for you to say to the children. The following steps will help you prepare.

Step 1: Quick Overview. Read the Memory Verse, Biblical Truth, and Teaching Tips.

Step 2: Bible Passage and Biblical Commentary. Read the verses in the Bible study passage, the information in the Biblical Commentary, and any Words of Our Faith.

Step 3: Activity. This section includes a game or other activity to prepare the children for the biblical lesson. Become familiar with the activity, the instructions, and the supplies. Bring any necessary supplies to the class with you. Set up the activity before the children arrive.

Step 4: Biblical Lesson. Review the lesson and learn it so that you can tell it as a story. A simple version of the scripture passage is included at the end of this book to help you prepare. The children want the teacher to tell the story rather than read it from the book. Use the Words of Our Faith from each lesson to provide additional information as you tell the story. After the story, use the review questions. They will help the children to understand the story and to apply it to their lives.

Step 5: Memory Verse. Learn the memory verse before you teach it to the children. A list of the memory verses and suggested memory verse activities are on pages 108-111. Choose from the activities to help the children to learn the memory verse. Become familiar with the activity that you choose. Read the instructions and prepare the supplies that you will bring to class.

Step 6: Additional Activities. The additional activities are an optional part of the study. These activities will enhance the children's biblical study. Many of these activities require additional supplies, resources, and time. Become familiar with the activities that you choose. Read the instructions and prepare the supplies that you will bring to class.

Step 7: Quizzing Practice. Quizzing is the competition part of *Bible Studies for Children* and you will find more information in the section called "Children's Bible Quizzing" (page 143).

Quizzing is an optional part of the study. If you choose to participate in quizzing, spend time with the children in their preparation. There are practice questions for each study. The first ten questions are for a basic level of competition. The questions are simple, and there are three possible answers for each question. The next ten questions are for an advanced level of the competition. There are four possible answers for each question, and these questions are more comprehensive. Children, with the guidance from their teacher, choose their level for the competition. Based on the number of children and the resources that are available, you may choose to offer only the basic level or only the advanced level. Before you ask the practice questions, read the scripture passage to the children.

STUDY 1

Genesis 1:1-31; 2:2-3, 7
In the Beginning

Memory Verse

"In the beginning God created the heavens and the earth." (Genesis 1:1).

Biblical Truth

God is the creator of the world.

Teaching Tip

As you lead the Bible study, remember that the power of God the Creator and the uniqueness of the people he created are the most important ideas of this study

BIBLICAL COMMENTARY

Creation displays the power of God. God spoke the words, and the lifeless planet responded. God's creation brought life out of emptiness and order from chaos. God called to creation and creation responded. This is God's first commandment.

God invited creation to come into being for delight and enjoyment, and "it was so". Similarly, creation eagerly responded with gratitude and delight.

Genesis 1:26-27 refers to the involvement of God the Father, the Son, and the Holy Spirit in creation.

God did not create everything haphazardly. Instead, everything has a purpose. People are most happy when they serve a noble purpose or work for something greater than themselves. In Genesis 2 and 3, we learn that God trusted the man and woman to take care of his special garden. This was an important task. It was not drudgery for Adam and Eve. They were content with their job.

From the beginning, God acted for the good of creation. To the man he gave a beautiful home and good food. He gave a caretaker to the garden. He warned Adam of the danger. He gave a helper to Adam.

God also set an example for people by resting on the seventh day. This does not imply that God was tired. Creation was complete, and God was content with what he created. He is also satisfied when the creation turns its attention to the creator. When Christians observe the Sabbath, it indicates their faith and trust in God. Resting reminds us, the created, to submit our will to God, the creator.

WORDS OF OUR FAITH

man -- humanity. God made a male and a female. Together he called them man or mankind. They were both created in the image of God.

ACTIVITY

Before the children arrive, choose an outside location for this activity. You will lead the children on a nature walk to this location. Find a space for the children to sit so that they will be able to discuss what they see.

During the class, say, **Today we will take a nature walk. As we walk, look at everything around you. Think about what you see: the sky, the grass, the flowers, the birds, the animals, and the people.**

Lead the children to the location you chose. Encourage the children to share with the class the things they saw as they walked.

Say, **The Bible is a book that tells the story of God. The book of Genesis tells us that God created the world. God created the ground where we sit. He created the sky above our heads. God created the plants, the trees, and the flowers. God created the animals. He also created people.**

Pray with the children. Thank God for everything he created. In your prayer, say the name of each child and thank God for him or her.

Return to the classroom.

BIBLICAL LESSON

Prepare a Bible story based on the lesson's scripture verses. Children will understand the lesson better if you tell them the story rather than reading it to them. A simpler version of this story is printed in the back of this book, on pages 112-113. This story is easier to read and understand.

After the story, encourage the children to discuss the story by asking the following questions. This will help them apply it to their lives. There may not be a right or wrong answer.

1. **What would you say to God if you watched him create everything on the earth?**
2. **How did God create people differently from the rest of creation? How does that difference make you feel about God?**
3. **God set the example for us on the seventh day. He rested. Do you like to rest? Do you think it is important? Why or why not?**
4. **What is the most important idea in the memory verse, Genesis 1:1?**

Say, **Close your eyes and think about your favourite animal, your favourite colour, your favourite fruit, your best friend, and a family member. God created col-**

9

ours, plants, animals, and people.

God is powerful and creative. The Bible says that God cares for everything he made. God made people. God created people to have a relationship with him. You can praise God because he is the Creator of the entire universe, and he cares for you.

MEMORY VERSE

Practice the study's memory verse. You will find suggestions for memory verse activities on pages 110-111.

ADDITIONAL ACTIVITIES

Choose from these options to enhance the children's Bible study.

1. Create an art project about creation, including papier-mâché models, clay figures, dioramas, paintings, posters, murals, or chalk drawings. Provide the children with a variety of craft supplies. Encourage the children to be creative.
2. Ask the children about how God created the world. Then, discuss with them why it is more important that we understand the one who created everything is more important than how it was done.

QUESTIONS FOR BASIC COMPETITION

To prepare the children for competition, read Genesis 1:1-31; 2:2-3, 7 to them.

1 Who created the heavens and the earth? (1:1)
1. Man
2. **God**
3. No one

2 What did God create on the first day? (1:3, 5)
1. Sea life
2. Plants and trees
3. **Light**

3 What did God do on the second day? (1:7-8)
1. Created the stars
2. **Separated the waters**
3. Created man

4 What did God tell the land to produce on the third day? (1:11, 13)
1. Livestock and wild animals
2. **Trees and plants**
3. Both answers are correct.

5 Why did God create the greater lights and the lesser lights? (1:14-18)
1. To separate the day from the night
2. To mark the seasons
3. **Both answers are correct.**

6 When did God create birds? (1:20, 23)
1. The third day
2. The fourth day
3. **The fifth day**

7 How did God create man? (1:26-27)
1. From the water of the ocean
2. From the clouds of the sky
3. **In the image of God**

8 What did God give to the man and the woman to eat? (1:29)
1. Meat
2. **Seed-bearing plants and fruit**
3. Both answers are correct.

9 What did God do on the seventh day? (2:2-3)
1. God blessed the day and called it holy.
2. God rested.
3. **Both answers are correct.**

10 From what did God form man? (2:7)
1. **From the dust of the ground**
2. From the air
3. Both answers are correct.

QUESTIONS FOR ADVANCED COMPETITION

To prepare the children for competition, read Genesis 1:1-31; 2:2-3, 7 to them.

1 What was the earth like before creation? (1:2)
1. Formless
2. Empty
3. Covered in darkness
4. All of the answers are correct.

2 What happened to the waters on the third day? (1:9-11)
1. They dried up.
2. They gathered in the sky.
3. They were gathered in one place as seas.
4. All of the answers are correct.

3 What did God create on the fourth day? (1:16, 19)
1. Sun, moon, and stars
2. Plants and trees
3. Birds and sea life
4. Animals and people

4 On the sixth day, what did God create according to their kinds? (1:25)
1. Wild animals
2. Livestock
3. All the creatures that move along the ground
4. All of the answers are correct.

5 In whose image did God create man? (1:26)
1. Animals
2. God
3. The earth
4. The sky

6 When God created man and woman, what did he say to them? (1:28)
1. "Fill the earth and subdue it."
2. "Rule over the fish of the sea, the birds of the air, and over every living creature that lives on the ground."
3. "Be fruitful and increase in number."
4. All of the answers are correct.

7 What did God give to the man and woman to eat? (1:29)
1. Seed-bearing plants and fruit
2. Birds
3. Animals
4. All of the answers are correct.

8 Finish this verse, "God saw all that he had made . . ." (1:31)
1. ". . . and he was sad."
2. ". . . and he needed rest."
3. ". . . and it was very good."
4. All of the answers are correct.

9 Why did God bless the seventh day and make it holy? (2:3)
1. He needed a break.
2. He rested on this day from all the work of creating he had done.
3. He could not think of anything else to create.
4. He wanted to go to church.

10 From what did God form man? (2:7)
1. The dust of the ground
2. The air
3. The water
4. The plants

STUDY 2

The Problem of Sin

Memory Verse

"So God created mankind in his own image, in the image of God he created them; male and female he created them." (Genesis 1:27)

Biblical Truth

God wants to have a close relationship with us.

Teaching Tip

As you lead the Bible study, focus on Adam and Eve's desire for knowledge rather than trust.

BIBLICAL COMMENTARY

Adam and Eve were part of God's creation and lived in a close relationship with God. Adam and Eve used their God-given ability to make choices. However, Adam and Eve made a poor choice, and they suffered the consequences of their choice. They were no longer allowed to live in the goodness of the garden.

When we choose our own way rather than the way of God, we experience guilt, and our selfishness is exposed. Often, we attempt to hide from God, but this does not make our pitiful situation better. Only God can bring reconciliation. He makes this possible through his prevenient grace.

Prevenient grace is when God acts on our behalf or reaches out to us before we even think about him or ask him for anything. Grace means "gift of God." Prevenient grace makes it possible for us to want to seek God.

People have the freedom to choose between right and wrong. Because sin is such a big part of our world, we most often choose wrongly. This is not the type of world God intended. He is working through people to set things right. God's prevenient grace encourages us to draw near to him instead.

WORDS OF OUR FAITH

to sin -- to disobey God. We sin when we put our will above God's will. Sin can refer to a person's nature or to an action. We sin when we do something that God said not to do. We also sin when we fail to do what God said to do.

ACTIVITY

You will need these items for this activity:

- some small pieces of paper
- a large piece of paper and a marker. If you have access to a board, then you need to have chalk or a marker.
- question cards (see below for instructions)
- tape to affix the cards to the board

Before class, draw a large fruit tree on the board.

To prepare question cards, write the number "100" on a card or piece of paper. Write the number "200" on another card, then write the number "300" on another card. Continue this pattern (100, 200, 300) for each question. On the other side of each card, write one of the questions that follow. You may want to write a few more questions of your own to give children more opportunities. Attach these cards to the tree with only the number side of the card showing.

Say, **Today you will learn about Adam, Eve, the serpent, and the choices that Adam and Eve made. Each team may pick a "fruit" from the tree. If you answer the question on the paper correctly, your team will receive the points indicated on that paper.**

Divide the group into two teams and begin the game. Encourage the children to help their teammates answer the questions. Keep score of the points.

Questions:

1. **Who created the world?** (God)
2. **What did God call the dry ground?** (land)
3. **What did God call the gathered waters?** (seas)
4. **What did God breathe into the first man?** (breath of life)
5. **When did God create the animals?** (the sixth day)
6. **From what did God make the man?** (the dust of the ground)
7. **What did God create on the seventh day?** (nothing, he rested; he created the Sabbath, a day for rest)
8. **In whose image did God create the people?** (in his image)

BIBLICAL LESSON

Prepare a Bible story based on the lesson's scripture verses. Children will understand the lesson better if you tell them the story rather than reading it to them. A simpler version of this story is printed in the back of this book, on pages 113-116. This story is easier to read and understand.

After the story, encourage the children

to discuss the story by asking the following questions. This will help them apply it to their lives. There may not be a right or wrong answer.

1. **What did Adam and Eve do when they heard God in the garden? Have you ever tried to hide from someone after you disobeyed? How did you feel?**
2. **Who or what is cursed because of the actions of Adam and Eve? Do you think sin affects only the person who committed the sin? Explain your answer.**
3. **Why did God banish the couple from the garden?**
4. **How does today's memory verse, Genesis 1:27, relate to this story and to our lives?**

Say, **God created all things for good purposes. But Adam and Eve chose not to trust God. They thought they knew what was best. So, they disobeyed God. Adam and Eve made a bad decision, and that is bad news. The good news is that God wanted to repair his relationship with Adam and Eve. God does that with us too. Even when we disobey God, God wants to repair the relationship. If God can work with Adam and Eve, God can work with you.**

MEMORY VERSE

Practice the study's memory verse. You will find suggestions for memory verse activities on pages 110-111.

ADDITIONAL ACTIVITIES

Choose from these options to enhance the children's Bible study.

1. Ask, **What are some freedoms your parents allow you now? How can your choices influence your freedoms?** Together with the class, create a chart with three columns. In the middle, record a list of freedoms the children have. On the left, write down choices which may negatively affect their freedom. On the right, record choices which may positively affect their freedom. Say, **Let us ask God to help us to make choices that he thinks are best.**
2. Use modern maps to find the Tigris and Euphrates Rivers. Ask, **Can you guess where the Garden of Eden may have been?** (Some scholars suggest southern Iraq, but no one knows for sure.)

QUESTIONS FOR BASIC COMPETITION

To prepare the children for competition, read Genesis 2:15-25; 3:1-24 to them.

1 What was Adam's job in the Garden of Eden? (2:15-20)

1. He worked and cared for the garden
2. He named all the animals.
3. **Both answers are correct.**

2 Why did God create a woman for the man? (2:18, 20)

1. **It was not good for the man to be alone.**
2. Adam did not like any of the animals.
3. Both answers are correct.

3 What did the serpent say to Eve about God's commands? (3:1)

1. "It is OK to eat from any tree."
2. "God wanted me to tell you not to eat any fruit."
3. **"Did God really say, 'You must not eat from any tree in the garden'?"**

4 Who was the first to eat the fruit? (3:6)

1. The serpent
2. The man
3. **The woman**

5 Why did Adam and Eve hide from God? (3:8-10)

1. They were afraid because they stole the fruit.
2. **They were afraid because they were naked.**
3. Both answers are correct.

6 Whom did the man blame when God asked if he ate from the tree? (3:11-12)

1. **The woman (Eve)**
2. Himself
3. The serpent

7 What happened to the serpent (3:14)

1. God blessed the serpent.
2. **God cursed the serpent.**
3. The woman cared for the serpent.

8 How did Adam obtain the garments of animal skins? (3:21)

1. **God made them.**
2. Adam made them.
3. Eve made them.

9 What happened after God made garments for Adam and Eve?

1. God said, "The man has now become like one of us."
2. God banished them from the Garden of Eden.
3. **Both answers are correct.**

10 With what did God guard the way to the tree of life? (3:24)

1. The serpent
2. **The cherubim and a flaming sword**
3. Both answers are correct

QUESTIONS FOR ADVANCED COMPETITION

To prepare the children for competition, read Genesis 2:15-25; 3:1-24 to them.

1 Why did God put the man in the garden? (2:15)

1. **To work and care for the garden**
2. To protect the woman from the animals
3. The rest of the world was unformed
4. All of the answers are correct.

2 From what did God form the woman? (2:21-22)

1. The air
2. The water
3. **One of Adam's ribs**
4. Nothing

3 Who asked, "Did God really say, 'You must not eat from any tree in the garden?'" (3:1)

1. **The serpent**
2. The woman
3. The man
4. The cherubim

4 What did the serpent say would happen if the woman ate from the tree in the middle of the garden? (3:2-5)

1. Her eyes would be opened.
2. She would be like God.
3. She would know good and evil.
4. **All of the answers are correct.**

5 When did the man and the woman realize that they were naked? (3:6-7)

1. When the serpent told them
2. When God called for them in the garden
3. **After they ate the fruit**
4. All of the answers are correct.

6 What happened because of Adam and Eve's disobedience? (3:14-19)

1. God banished them from the garden.
2. God cursed the ground.
3. The woman would have pain in childbearing.
4. **All of the answers are correct.**

7 Why did Adam name the woman Eve? (3:20)

1. Because she was beautiful
2. **Because she would become the mother of all the living**
3. Because it was his favourite name
4. Because they lived in the Garden of Eden

8 What happened after God made garments for Adam and Eve? (3:21-24)

1. God clothed them.
2. They were banished from the Garden of Eden.
3. God placed the cherubim on the east side of the garden.
4. **All of the answers are correct.**

9 Why did God place the cherubim and the flaming sword on the east side of the garden? (3:24)

1. Because he was afraid
2. **To guard the way to the tree of life**
3. To prune the trees there
4. All of the answers are correct.

10 Finish this verse: "So God created mankind in his own image, in the image of God he created them; . . ." (Genesis 1:27)

1. **". . . male and female he created them."**
2. ". . . then he created woman."
3. ". . . female and male were created equal."
4. ". . . and then God rested."

STUDY 3

Genesis 4:1-16, 25-26
Cain's Conflict

Memory Verse

"But if you do not do what is right, sin is crouching at your door; it desires to have you, but you must rule over it." (Genesis 4:7b)

Biblical Truth

God is both holy and merciful.

Teaching Tip

Abel's name means "vapour" or "nothingness". Cain and God are the main characters of the story. Help the children to follow the dialog between Cain and God.

BIBLICAL COMMENTARY

Cain and Abel lived outside of the Garden of Eden. Abel became a shepherd and tended flocks, while Cain became a farmer. The Bible does not say why Cain's offering displeased God. However, the Bible does make it clear that Cain had the opportunity to make a right choice. Cain was free and capable of faithfulness.

Verses five and six define Cain's source of trouble. He was angry. But Cain was not angry at his brother for bringing the sacrifice of the firstborn flock. No, he was angry at God for not accepting his offering of fruits of the soil. God acted in a way that Cain did not understand. However God reminded Cain that he had a choice. He could change his attitude toward God and his brother and do well. Or he could succumb to his anger.

In verse seven, the Bible uses vivid imagery to describe sin. This verse compares sin to a predator stalking its prey. Sin is portrayed in this passage as conniving and vicious. God warned Cain that his thoughts and anger were dangerous. Unfortunately, Cain did not listen to God. He chose instead to give in to his thoughts of destruction.

At the end of the story, Cain is marked by God. This mark indicates Cain's guilt. However, it is also a sign of God's mercy. God spared his life by keeping anyone from killing him.

WORDS OF OUR FAITH

to show mercy -- to extend forgiveness or kindness to someone who has done wrong.

ACTIVITY

You will need the following items for this activity:

- stackable blocks (wooden or cardboard)
- small pieces of paper
- a pen or a pencil
- clear tape

Before class, write the following words on small pieces of paper: selfishness, anger, and jealousy. Make several sets. Make a tower with the stackable blocks. Tape the pieces of paper with words on them to several of the blocks.

Say, **Today we will learn how wrong attitudes can affect relationships. Each person will receive an opportunity to remove a block. How many blocks can we remove and keep the tower standing?**

Play a few rounds. Say, **Some blocks had words on them. What were they?** Allow children to respond. **Today we will learn about Cain. Cain struggled with wrong attitudes, such as anger, selfishness, and jealousy. These attitudes ruin relationships. When you removed blocks from the tower, it fell. When a person has wrong attitudes, they ruin the relationship with God.**

BIBLICAL LESSON

Prepare a Bible story based on the lesson's scripture verses. Children will understand the lesson better if you tell them the story rather than reading it to them. A simpler version of this story is printed in the back of this book, on page 116. This story is easier to read and understand.

After the story, encourage the children to discuss the story by asking the following questions. This will help them apply it to their lives. There may not be a right or wrong answer.

1. Why was Cain angry?

2. God helped Cain to see that he had a choice regarding his attitude. If Cain changed his attitude, how would the story be different?

3. Have you ever struggled with jealousy or anger in your family? How did you deal with it?

4. How does today's memory verse, Genesis 4:7b, relate to this story and to your life?

Cain had a bad attitude. He did not ask God to forgive him. Instead, Cain vented his anger on his brother. God punished Cain because he killed Abel. The Bible says not to sin "in your anger" (see Ephesians 4:26)**. That means, if you are angry, do not act out your anger and hurt someone or yourself. Cain had the opportunity to ask God for help, but he did not. God knows that we struggle with anger and jealousy, and God wants to help us overcome these problems.**

MEMORY VERSE

Practice the study's memory verse. You will find suggestions for memory verse activities on pages 110-111.

ADDITIONAL ACTIVITIES

Choose from these options to enhance the children's Bible study.

1. Research various Old Testament worship and sacrifice rituals. Read Leviticus 1—7 to learn about these sacrificial offerings and their meanings: burnt offering, grain offering, fellowship offering, and sin offering.

2. Discuss this question: Who suffers most from feelings of anger and hate? Is it you or the person whom you hate? When you are angry, what happens to your stomach and intestines? Is this good for your body? What could happen to your body after a long period of time? What could you do instead of hating?

QUESTIONS FOR BASIC COMPETITION

To prepare the children for competition, read Genesis 4:1-16, 25-26 to them.

1 Who was the oldest son of Adam and Eve? (4:1-2)
   1. Abel
   2. Seth
   3. Cain

2 What was Cain's job? (4:2)
   1. Shepherd
   2. Farmer
   3. Fisherman

3 What was Abel's job? (4:2)
   1. Fisherman
   2. Farmer
   3. Shepherd

4 Who pleased the Lord with his offering? (4:4)
   1. Cain
   2. Adam
   3. Abel

5 What made Cain angry? (4:4-5)
   1. The Lord did not look with favour on his offering.
   2. The Lord looked with favour on Abel's offering.
   3. Both answers are correct.

6 What did the Lord say that Cain must master? (4:7)
   1. Gardening
   2. Sin
   3. Both answers are correct.

7 Why did the Lord punish Cain? (4:8-11)
   1. Cain attacked and killed Abel.
   2. Cain offered fish to the Lord.
   3. Cain did not want to be a farmer.

8 What was Cain's punishment? (4:11-12)
   1. The ground would not grow crops for him.
   2. He could never leave the Garden of Eden.
   3. Both answers are correct.

9 Where did Cain go when he left the garden? (4:16)
   1. The land of Nod
   2. East of Eden
   3. Both answers are correct.

10 When did people begin to call on the name of the Lord? (4:26)
   1. When they heard that Abel was dead
   2. Before Abel was born
   3. About the time that Seth's son was born

QUESTIONS FOR ADVANCED COMPETITION

To prepare children for competition, read Genesis 4:1-16, 25-26 to them.

1 What is the right order of birth of the three sons of Adam and Eve? (4:1-2, 25)
1. Abel, Seth, and Cain
2. **Cain, Abel, and Seth**
3. Abel, Cain, and Seth
4. None of the above

2 What did Cain bring as an offering? (4:3)
1. Fat portions of the firstborn of his flock
2. His brother's offering
3. **Some of the fruits of the soil**
4. All of the answers are correct.

3 What did Abel bring as an offering? (4:4)
1. **Fat portions of the firstborn of his flock**
2. Some of the fruits of the soil
3. His brother
4. All of the answers are correct.

4 On whose offering did the Lord look with favour? (4:4-5)
1. Cain's offering
2. **Abel's offering**
3. Both offerings
4. Neither offering

5 What did the Lord say about the sin that crouched at Cain's door? (4:7)
1. Sin would be no problem for Cain.
2. Sin already mastered Cain.
3. **Sin desired to have Cain, but he must rule over it.**
4. All of the answers are correct.

6 What did Cain say when the Lord asked where Abel was? (4:9)
1. "He's in the pasture with the sheep."
2. "He's with our parents."
3. "He's with me in the garden."
4. **"I don't know. Am I my brother's keeper?"**

7 How did God punish Cain for killing Abel? (4:11-12)
1. **God expelled him from his home, and crops would not grow for him.**
2. The Lord did not protect Cain from those who wanted to hurt him.
3. Cain would never be around other people.
4. All of the answers are correct.

8 What did Cain say to the Lord after he received his punishment? (4:13)
1. "Thank you for having mercy on me."
2. "I did not mean to kill my brother."
3. **"My punishment is more than I can bear."**
4. "I will not accept this punishment."

9 What would happen to anyone who tried to kill Cain? (4:15)
1. Nothing
2. **That person would suffer vengeance seven times more.**
3. The Lord would bless that person.
4. That person would suffer vengeance ten times more.

10 Finish this verse: "But if you do not do what is right, sin is crouching at your door; it desires to have you, ..." (4:7b).
1. " . . . so let it have you."
2. " . . . but you must trust in the Lord."
3. **" . . . but you must rule over it."**
4. " . . . so do as you please."

STUDY 4

Memory Verse

"Noah was a righteous man, blameless among the people of his time, and he walked faithfully with God." (Genesis 6:9b)

Biblical Truth

God is with you, even if you think that you are the only person who obeys him.

Teaching Tip

•As you lead the Bible study, focus on Noah's response to God's instructions.
•Remind the children that obeying God is worth the risk of looking foolish.

BIBLICAL COMMENTARY

The story of Noah and the flood is one of the most well-known stories of the Bible. Genesis 6 describes a time when the people were very evil and wicked. When God looked into the heart of mankind, he saw "only evil all the time." Verse six says that the heart of the Lord was "deeply troubled." The wickedness of mankind pained God's heart. God would not tolerate this wretched creation as it was. He would blot out the corruption and the violence. God's creation had no regard for him and were going their own way. God judged and condemned the earth.

However, at this point in the story where God lost hope for the world, Genesis 6:8 includes a critical transitional statement: "But Noah found favour in the eyes of the Lord." Because of Noah, another plan was possible. God invited Noah to be a part of it. God told Noah the plan and gave Noah specific instructions. This time God attempted a new covenant with the only one who continued to walk with him. Thanks to Noah's righteousness, he and his family were spared.

So while all of creation was perverse, God found someone who still followed him. In verses 6:22 and 7:5 we discover the character of Noah as he listened and obeyed. God changed his position toward humanity.

WORDS OF OUR FAITH

righteous -- to be in right relationship with God and to obey him because of that relationship. To be righteous is to be like Christ in thoughts, words, and actions.

ACTIVITY

You will need these items for this activity:
- a tape measure
- four pylons or some other objects to mark the corners of the ark
- a very large area
- small pieces of paper
- a pen or a pencil

Before class, if possible, find an area to measure and mark the size of Noah's ark. Use pylons or other objects to mark the corners of the area. The ark was approximately 140 meters long, 23 meters wide, and 13.5 meters high. If this is not possible, measure the size of your space and determine what fraction your space is when compared to the size of the ark.

Write the name of an animal on two separate pieces of paper. Repeat this until you have several pairs of animals. Plan for each child to have one piece of paper.

To begin the class, tell the children the size of the ark. Say, **Today, we are going to learn about Noah and the ark. The ark was huge! It was bigger than a soccer field! We will find out why it was so big.**

Distribute to each child a piece of paper with the name of an animal. Tell the children to read silently the name of the animal and to keep it a secret. If you have children who cannot read yet, whisper the name of the animal to them. When you give the signal, the children will make the sound of their animal and try to find their partner, the other child with the same animal name.

After the children have found their animal partner, if possible, take time to walk around the perimeter of the area to allow children to get an idea of how large the ark was. Tell the children what fraction your space is when compared to the ark.

BIBLICAL LESSON

Prepare a Bible story based on the lesson's scripture verses. Children will understand the lesson better if you tell them the story rather than reading it to them. A simpler version of this story is printed in the back of this book, on pages 117-118. This story is easier to read and understand.

After the story, encourage the children to discuss the story by asking the following questions. This will help them apply it to their lives. There may not be a right or wrong answer.

1. **How was Noah different from the other people?**
2. **How is your neighbourhood similar or different from the place where Noah lived?**
3. **How would you react if God asked you to do something like building an ark?**
4. **Tell about a time when you thought**

you were the only person who wanted to do the right thing.

Say, **It is difficult to do the right thing when no one else does it. Noah probably felt that way. Noah loved God and wanted to please him, but the other people did not care about God. Noah thought he was alone. Did God notice that Noah always tried to do the right thing? The Bible says that he did. God helped Noah to prepare for the flood, and all of Noah's family survived.**

God does notice our efforts to love him and to do the right thing. We need to love and serve God regardless of the attitudes of other people.

MEMORY VERSE

Practice the study's memory verse. You will find suggestions for memory verse activities on pages 110-111

ADDITIONAL ACTIVITIES

Choose from these options to enhance the children's Bible study.

1. Study more about Noah's ark. Ask the children to draw an ark. Help them design space inside for the animals to live, the people to live, and other things like food and water storage.
2. Make a small model of the ark from papier-mâché or clay.
3. Write a drama about the conversations between Noah and his sons as they built the ark.

QUESTIONS FOR BASIC COMPETITION

To prepare the children for competition, read Genesis 6:5-7:16 to them.

1 What had become great on the earth? (6:5)

    1. Man's wickedness

    2. Man's goodness

    3. The Bible does not say.

2 What kind of man was Noah? (6:9)

    1. Righteous

    2. Blameless

    3. Both answers are correct.

3 Why did God tell Noah to build an ark? (6:13-14)

    1. The Lord would destroy the people and the earth.

    2. The Lord said a great earthquake was coming.

    3. Both answers are correct.

4 Who did the Lord say could go on the ark with Noah? (6:18)

    1. Noah's wife

    2. Noah's sons and their wives

    3. Both answers are correct.

5 How did Noah find the animals to put on the ark? (6:20)

    1. His sons went out and found all the animals.

    2. The animals came to Noah.

    3. The Lord sent all the animals to a river.

6 How long did the Lord say it would rain? (7:4)

    1. For 40 days and 40 nights

    2. For 7 days and 7 nights

    3. For two weeks

7 How much of what the Lord commanded him did Noah do? (7:5)

    1. All of what God commanded

    2. Some of what God commanded

    3. None of what God commanded

8 How old was Noah when he entered the ark? (7:11, 13)

    1. 500 years old

    2. 600 years old

    3. 700 years old

9 What happened on the day the rain started? (7:13-15)

    1. Noah allowed some neighbours to go into the ark.

    2. The people asked for forgiveness from God.

    3. Noah and his family entered the ark with the animals.

10 After the animals entered, who shut Noah in? (7:16)

    1. Noah

    2. The Lord

    3. His sons

QUESTIONS FOR ADVANCED COMPETITION

To prepare children for competition, read Genesis 6:5-7:16 to them.

1 What were the people like during Noah's life? (6:5)
  1. They loved and worshiped God.
  2. They were wicked, and their thoughts were evil.
  3. They were all farmers.
  4. The Bible does not say.

2 How does the Bible describe Noah? (6:9)
  1. Righteous
  2. Blameless
  3. He walked with God.
  4. All of the answers are correct.

3 What were the names of Noah's sons? (6:10)
  1. Shem, Cain, Jacob
  2. Ham, Shem, Japheth
  3. Japheth, Joshua, Jacob
  4. All of the answers are correct.

4 How did the Lord destroy the earth? (6:17)
  1. A famine
  2. An earthquake
  3. Floodwaters
  4. Tornadoes

5 Who entered the ark? (6:18)
  1. Noah's sons and their wives
  2. Noah
  3. Noah's wife
  4. All of the answers are correct.

6 What did Noah do after God gave him the instructions for the ark? (7:5)
  1. Noah laughed and did nothing.
  2. Noah did all that the Lord commanded him.
  3. Noah instructed his sons to do the work.
  4. Noah asked for more information.

7 How old was Noah when he entered the ark? (7:6)
  1. 600 years old
  2. 500 years old
  3. 400 years old
  4. 300 years old

8 What entered the ark with Noah and his family? (7:13-15)
  1. Every wild animal and all livestock
  2. Every bird
  3. Pairs of all creatures that have the breath of life in them
  4. All of the answers are correct.

9 Who shut Noah in the ark? (7:16)
  1. The Lord
  2. Noah
  3. The people of Noah's generation
  4. Noah's sons

10 Finish this verse: "Noah was a righteous man, blameless among the people of his time, and he . . ." (Genesis 6:9b)
  1. ". . . did everything God asked him to do."
  2. ". . . had no sin."
  3. ". . . walked faithfully with God."
  4. ". . . built an ark."

STUDY 5

Memory Verse

"As long as the earth endures, seedtime and harvest, cold and heat, summer and winter, day and night will never cease." (Genesis 8:22)

Biblical Truth

God will help you to do the things he asks.

Teaching Tip

• As you lead the Bible study, focus on the chronological facts of the Flood and God's authority over the earth.

• If your church has an altar, make arrangements to have the children view the altar and talk about its significance. Discuss the difference in how altars were used in the Old Testament as opposed to how we use them today (see Romans 12:1).

BIBLICAL COMMENTARY

The Flood is one of the most exciting and dramatic accounts in the Bible. The story gives valuable insight into how God interacts with people.

God created people in his image for the purpose of having a special and unique relationship with them. This relationship deteriorated quickly with the disobedience of Adam and Eve. As the generations of people began to fill the earth, so did the rebellion, violence and sin.

However, God still loved people. God was especially pleased with Noah. "Noah found favour in the eyes of the Lord." The interaction between Noah and God helps us to understand the power of obedience to God's instructions.

God's act of mercy to Noah and his family provides for us an insight about the nature of God. God created the world, and he had the authority to destroy it. Yet, because he highly values relationships, he saved the human race from being totally destroyed. This shows God's unfailing love and mercy.

WORDS OF OUR FAITH

sovereign -- the power to rule with no limitation. A sovereign king is not controlled by any other person or nation.

an altar -- a structure built by people in the Old Testament to offer sacrifices to God. To offer a sacrifice was a way that people worshipped God. Today, some churches have altars so that people can have a special place to talk to God.

a sacrifice -- something valuable that is offered to God. In Old Testament times, the sacrifice was usually an animal, some fruit, or some grain. In Romans 12:1-2, the Bible tells us that we can offer our lives to be used according to God's purposes.

ACTIVITY

You will need these items for this activity:
- white paper or cardstock
- crayons

After you tell the story, gather children into groups of five. Remind the children of the main points of the story: **1) flood waters rose, 2) God remembered Noah, 3) the ark landed on Mount Ararat, 4) Noah sent out a dove to look for dry ground 5) Noah built an altar to worship God.**

Distribute five pieces of paper to each group. Ask children in each group to decide who will draw these images: water, Noah, mountain, dove, altar. (Note: an altar can be drawn as a cairn or neatly stacked rocks.)

When the children finish the drawings, instruct them to put the pictures in order and retell the story using their images. Each child may tell the part of the story he or she drew. If time permits, have children switch cards and tell the story again.

Say, **The rising waters must have frightened Noah and his family. But God did not forget his promise. He remembered Noah. When you are worried about something, know that God remembers you too!**

BIBLICAL LESSON

Prepare a Bible story based on the lesson's scripture verses. Children will understand the lesson better if you tell them the story rather than reading it to them. A simpler version of this story is printed in the back of this book, on pages 118-119. This story is easier to read and understand.

After the story, encourage the children to discuss the story by asking the following questions. This will help them apply it to their lives. There may not be a right or wrong answer.

1. **Noah and his family waited for 40 days while the flood waters rose. Then they waited 150 days more. Then they waited, and waited and waited for the waters to recede. Have you ever had to wait for something? How did that make you feel?**
2. **What do you think Noah and his family did while they waited inside of the ark?**
3. **After Noah left the ark, how did he thank God?**
4. **Name something for which you can thank God.**
5. **How does the memory verse, Genesis 8:22, relate to this story?**

Say, **There are many opportunities for**

adults to serve God. What can a child do?

Children can learn from Noah that God does not require them to leave where they live to serve him and obey him. Noah did what God asked him to do. Think about Noah when you ask, "What can I do to serve God?" Remind the children that the best way we can serve God is to obey him.

MEMORY VERSE

Practice the study's memory verse. You will find suggestions for memory verse activities on pages 110-111.

ADDITIONAL ACTIVITIES

Choose from these options to enhance the children's Bible study.

1. Research an altar. How did people use altars during Bible times? Find other scripture passages that talk about making an altar to God. Make a model of one.
2. Create a diorama of the ark resting on the mountains of Ararat.
3. Draw a picture of the ark and your favourite animal.

QUESTIONS FOR BASIC COMPETITION

To prepare the children for competition, read Genesis 7:17-8:22 to them.

1 How long did the rains last? (7:17)
1. 40 weeks
2. **40 days**
3. 40 hours

2 What happened when God sent the rains? (7:19-21)
1. Every living thing on the earth died.
2. Water covered even the highest mountains.
3. **Both answers are correct.**

3 Who remained alive on the earth? (7:23)
1. Noah
2. The people who were with Noah in the ark
3. **Both answers are correct.**

4 Where did the ark come to rest? (8:4)
1. **The mountains of Ararat**
2. The mountain of God
3. The Garden of Eden

5 After the rain stopped, which bird did Noah send out first? (8:7)
1. **A raven**
2. A dove
3. A pigeon

6 What did the dove bring back to Noah? (8:11)
1. A blade of grass
2. An apple
3. **A freshly plucked olive leaf**

7 When did Noah remove the covering from the ark? (8:13)
1. As soon as it stopped raining
2. **When the water had dried up from the earth**
3. Both answers are correct.

8 What did Noah do with the altar he built? (8:20)
1. **He sacrificed some clean animals and birds to the Lord.**
2. He sacrificed some unclean animals to the Lord.
3. He sacrificed olive trees and fruit to the Lord.

9 What did the Lord say he would never do again? (8:21)
1. Destroy all living creatures
2. Curse the ground because of man
3. **Both answers are correct.**

10 How long did God say that summer and winter would endure? (8:22)
1. Forever
2. **As long as the earth endures**
3. Until the next flood

QUESTIONS FOR ADVANCED COMPETITION

To prepare children for competition, read Genesis 7:17-8:22 to them.

1 What happened during the Flood? (7:17-23)
1. The waters rose more than 20 feet above the mountains.
2. All the living things outside the ark died.
3. It rained for 40 days.
4. **All of the answers are correct.**

2 How did the waters recede? (8:1)
1. **God sent a wind over the earth.**
2. The sun made all the water evaporate.
3. The earth swallowed the water.
4. The Bible does not say.

3 When did the ark come to rest on the mountains of Ararat? (8:4)
1. **The seventeenth day of the seventh month**
2. The seventh day of the seventeenth month
3. The second day of the seventeenth month
4. The seventh day of the second month

4 After the rain stopped, which bird did Noah send out first (8:6-7)
1. A parrot
2. An owl
3. A dove
4. **A raven**

5 How did Noah know that the water had receded from the earth? (8:11)
1. **The dove brought back a freshly plucked olive leaf.**
2. The dove did not return.
3. The raven brought back a leaf.
4. God told Noah the waters receded.

6 When did Noah first see that the surface of the ground was dry? (8:13)
1. He opened the door of the ark
2. **He removed the covering from the ark.**
3. The feet of the raven were not muddy.
4. There were no more leaks in the ark.

7 How did Noah know when to leave the ark? (8:15-16)
1. The sunlight began to warm the ark.
2. The birds became restless.
3. The animals began to attack each other.
4. **God told Noah to leave the ark.**

8 What did Noah do when he left the ark? (8:20)
1. He found new homes for the animals.
2. He built homes for the animals.
3. **He built an altar and offered burnt offerings to the Lord.**
4. All of the answers are correct.

9 What did the Lord say that he would never do again? (8:21)
1. Let the people become evil
2. Punish the people for their sin
3. **Curse the ground because of man and destroy all living creatures**
4. All of the answers are correct.

10 Finish this verse: "As long as the earth endures, seedtime and harvest, cold and heat, summer and winter, . . ." (Genesis 8:22)
1. ". . . I will praise the Lord."
2. **" . . . day and night will never cease."**
3. ". . . every season has its time."
4. " . . . will also endure."

STUDY 6

The Rainbow in the Clouds

Memory Verse

"I have set my rainbow in the clouds, and it will be the sign of the covenant between me and the earth." (Genesis 9:13)

Biblical Truth

God established a covenant with people.

Teaching Tip

As you lead the Bible study, focus on the ways that God changed after the flood and the promise signified by the rainbow.

BIBLICAL COMMENTARY

God confirms his covenant with Noah and honours Noah's obedience. God also initiates and honours a covenant with people. God maintains his covenant with humanity despite their unfaithfulness. The covenant between God, the earth, and its inhabitants is the final part of this dramatic story.

For the children to understand this resolution, it is important to understand what a covenant is. A covenant is a serious agreement between two people. In this case, the covenant is between God and the earth, the people, and all other life on the earth (the animals, the birds, and the fish). God said the rainbow was the sign of his covenant.

After the flood, God had different expectations for people. People are not restricted to a diet of fruit and vegetables. God allowed people also to eat the meat. However, God still put constraints on how his people should prepare the meat. For instance, they needed to drain the blood first. God still cares for people and he cares about how they live.

God does not tolerate sin. God will continue to work to make the world right. God does notice our efforts to serve him, and he honours those who obey him. Despite the wickedness of people, God still treasures those whom he created in his image.

WORDS OF OUR FAITH

a covenant -- a special, serious agreement between two people or between a person and God

ACTIVITY

You will need these items for this activity:

- six pieces of paper, each one coloured with a colour of the rainbow (red, orange, yellow, green, blue, purple).
- markers or crayons in the same colours
- a black marker or a crayon
- small pieces of paper, one for each child

To prepare, go to a large area and hide each coloured sheet of paper in a different place, along with the matching colour of marker or crayon. Choose one child to be the Rainbow Catcher, the player who tries to tag the other players and impede their progress.

To play, send out everyone except the Rainbow Catcher in search of the markers or crayons. Each time a child finds one of the markers or crayons, he or she should mark discreetly a stripe on his or her paper. The child should leave the marker or crayon in place. The Rainbow Catcher will try to tag the players. Every time he or she does, the Rainbow Catcher uses the black marker or crayon to eliminate one of the coloured stripes on the paper of the child. The first player to get one stripe in each colour wins.

Say, **That was a fun game, and it helped us to learn the colours of a rainbow. But, did you know there is more to a rainbow than just pretty colours? Today we will learn that God gave a special meaning to the rainbow.**

BIBLICAL LESSON

Prepare a Bible story based on the lesson's scripture verses. Children will understand the lesson better if you tell them the story rather than reading it to them. A simpler version of this story is printed in the back of this book, on pages 119-120. This story is easier to read and understand.

After the story, encourage the children to discuss the story by asking the following questions. This will help them apply it to their lives. There may not be a right or wrong answer.

1. **What do you think of when you see a rainbow?**
2. **How long are you able to keep a promise to your family or your friends? Could you keep a promise for eternity? What makes it difficult to keep a promise?**
3. **Noah was 950 years old. What do you think it would be like to be 950 years old? What changes might happen during your life?**
4. **How does the memory verse, Genesis 9:13, relate to this story?**

Say, **God's Word was true for the people in biblical times, and his Word is true** for us today. **God promised not to destroy the whole earth again with a flood. It was a promise to Noah, to his sons, and to all who came after them.**

When we see a rainbow in the sky, we remember God's promise to us. It is a sign of the covenant that God made with Noah long ago. God keeps his promises.

MEMORY VERSE

Practice the study's memory verse. You will find suggestions for memory verse activities on pages 110-111.

ADDITIONAL ACTIVITIES

Choose from these options to enhance the children's Bible study.

1. Discuss what a covenant is. A covenant can be a formal binding agreement that defines the relationships and the responsibilities between two or more people. There are four other major biblical covenants: the covenant with Abraham (Genesis 12); the covenant with Moses (Exodus 19 and 23); the covenant with David (2 Samuel 7); the new covenant (Luke 22:20). How are they alike? How are they different?

2. Ask the children to write letters to God, thanking him for keeping his covenant with people. Have the children include thanks to God for remembering his promise. If you have enough time and the children are interested, give them time to add some promises they will make to God also.

QUESTIONS FOR BASIC COMPETITION

To prepare the children for competition, read Genesis 9:1-20, 28-29 to them.

1 After he blessed them, what did God tell Noah and his sons to do? (9:1)

    1. Be fruitful and fill the earth.

    2. Rename the animals.

    3. Do not sin anymore.

2 What could people eat after the Flood? (9:3-4)

    1. Green plants

    2. Meat with no lifeblood

    3. Both answers are correct.

3 Why will God demand an accounting for the life of people? (9:5-6)

    1. Man is created in the image of God.

    2. Animals are more important than people.

    3. The Bible does not say.

4 What was the covenant that God made with all living creatures? (9:11)

    1. He will never again send a flood to destroy the earth and all life on it.

    2. He will no longer punish the people.

    3. He will never destroy the earth with fire.

5 What sign did God give for the covenant he made? (9:13)

    1. A rainbow

    2. The ark

    3. Both answers are correct.

6 How long did God say this covenant would last? (9:12)

    1. As long as Noah lived

    2. For all generations

    3. As long as Noah's sons lived

7 What will God remember when the rainbow appears? (9:16)

    1. The everlasting covenant he made

    2. The need for rain on the earth

    3. Both answers are correct.

8 From whom did all of the people come after the Flood? (9:19)

    1. Shem, Ham, and Japheth

    2. The sons of Abraham

    3. Both answers are correct.

9 For how many years did Noah live after the Flood? (9:28)

    1. 950 years

    2. 150 years

    3. 350 years

10 How old was Noah when he died? (9:29)

    1. 450 years

    2. 950 years

    3. 1050 years

QUESTIONS FOR ADVANCED COMPETITION

To prepare children for competition, read Genesis 9:1-20, 28-29 to them.

1 What did God tell Noah and his sons to do when they left the ark? (9:1)
1. Use the wood of the ark to build your houses.
2. **Be fruitful, increase in number, and fill the earth.**
3. Take care of the animals.
4. Plant crops and harvest them.

2 What was different about the earth and its inhabitants after the Flood? (9:2-5)
1. Animals were food for the people.
2. Animals were now afraid of the people.
3. God would demand an accounting from the people and the animals.
4. **All of the answers are correct.**

3 With whom did God establish the covenant? (9:9-10)
1. Noah
2. Noah's descendants
3. All the animals from the ark
4. **All of the answers are correct.**

4 What was the covenant that God established? (9:11)
1. He would never punish people again for their sin.
2. He would never allow people again to become wicked.
3. **He would never destroy again all life and the earth by a flood.**
4. He would never send again a rainbow on the earth.

5 Who would benefit from the covenant? (9:12)
1. **All of the generations to come**
2. Only one generation
3. Only the descendants of Ham
4. Only the descendants of Shem

6 What was the sign of the covenant? (9:13)
1. The Ten Commandments
2. Noah's three sons
3. A burnt offering
4. **A rainbow in the clouds**

7 What were the names of the sons of Noah? (9:18)
1. Shem, Joshua, and Moses
2. **Shem, Ham, and Japheth**
3. Ham, Japheth, and Samuel
4. Abraham, Isaac, and Jacob

8 From whom did the people come after the Flood? (9:19)
1. Adam
2. Eve
3. **Shem, Ham, and Japheth**
4. Noah's daughters

9 How old was Noah when he died? (9:29)
1. 350 years
2. 150 years
3. **950 years**
4. 600 years

10 Finish this verse: "I have set my rainbow in the clouds, and it will be a sign of the covenant between . . ." (Genesis 9:13)
1. **" . . . me and the earth."**
2. " . . . me and the animals."
3. " . . . me and your offspring."
4. " . . . me and Noah."

STUDY 7

Calls and Choices

"By faith Abraham, when called to go to a place he would later receive as his inheritance, obeyed and went, even though he did not know where he was going." (Hebrews 11:8)

Biblical Truth
You can trust God to do what he says.

Teaching Tip
Help children understand the value of trust in any relationship. Explain that when we make choices, we often do what we feel would be most beneficial to us personally. However, we can trust that God will lead us to do what is best for everyone.

BIBLICAL COMMENTARY

Abram's relationship with God was different from Lot's relationship with God. Abram and Lot made different choices and this study shows the results of those choices.

Lot and Abram left Haran with their families. When the new land could not support both families, Abram was gracious and offered Lot the first choice of land. Abram did not protect his own interest. Rather, he trusted God to bring him to the Promised Land and he was generous to Lot.

People often make choices based on what they think is best for them. God wants people to trust him and to choose his way. We cannot see into the future. Many times, we do not realize how it is possible for choices that we make today to affect the world tomorrow and in future years. However, God knows. So we should trust and obey God.

This lesson is a great opportunity to highlight Abram's faith. Abram's faith will affect the lives of his son (Isaac), his grandsons (Esau and Jacob), and even his great-grandson (Joseph).

ACTIVITY

You will need these items for this activity:
- 2 suitcases
- 2 sets of clothing (shirts, shoes)

- 2 sets of household items, to represent moving (pots, books, towels)
- 2 tables
- a stopwatch or a clock

Before class, arrange one suitcase, a set of clothing, and a set of household items on each table at the front of the room. The sets of clothing and household items should be equal in the quantity, the size, and the number of items. Provide enough items to make it a challenge to fit everything in the suitcases. Two children will race to find out who can be the first to pack everything in a suitcase.

Tell the children that you will give them 60 seconds to pack the suitcase. (It may take a longer time than this.) The goal is to be the first one to place everything in the suitcase and to close it. If time permits, let every child have an opportunity to pack a suitcase.

Say, **Today we will learn about some people who packed their belongings and moved to a new place. They had some tough decisions to make. We will learn how they responded to God's call to move.**

BIBLICAL LESSON

Prepare a Bible story based on the lesson's scripture verses. Children will understand the lesson better if you tell them the story rather than reading it to them. A simpler version of this story is printed in the back of this book, on pages 120-121. This story is easier to read and understand.

After the story, encourage the children to discuss the story by asking the following questions. This will help them apply it to their lives. There may not be a right or wrong answer.

1. **How would you respond if God asked you to leave your home and follow him? What would be the most difficult thing for you if God asked you to move?**
2. **Who do you think made a good choice in this story? Why?**
3. **Who do you think made a bad choice in this story? Why?**
4. **What does it mean to trust God?**
5. **Discuss today's memory verse, Hebrews 11:8. What did it mean for Abram to leave Haran? Do you know the story of anyone who had to trust God in a difficult situation?**

Say, **It can be difficult to make choices. Abram and Lot made some choices to settle the quarrels of their herdsmen. Out of respect for his uncle who was older, Lot should give Abram first choice. However, Lot chose first.**

Abram gave up the first choice because he had faith in God. Abram trusted God to help him on his journey. Abram trusted God to provide for his needs. And, Abram trusted God to do what God said that he would do.

MEMORY VERSE

Practice the study's memory verse. You will find suggestions for memory verse activities on pages 110-111.

ADDITIONAL ACTIVITIES

Choose from these options to enhance the children's Bible study.

1. Ask, **Have you ever moved to a new town? Write a story about your move. If you have not moved, pretend that you did. Include why you moved, what was easy and what was difficult about your move, and how you felt about it.**

2. Have the children draw a picture or make a scene that shows Lot and his herds on the plain of the Jordan River.

QUESTIONS FOR BASIC COMPETITION

To prepare the children for competition, read Genesis 12:1-9; 13:5-18 to them.

1 What did the Lord tell Abram to do? (12:1)
  1. **To go to a land that the Lord would show him.**
  2. To move to the sea.
  3. To stay in the land of his father.

2 Who went with Abram? (12:5)
  1. Sarai and Lot
  2. The people of his household
  3. **Both answers are correct.**

3 What did the Lord say that he would give to Abram's offspring? (12:6-7)
  1. The land where no one lived
  2. **The land of Canaan**
  3. Both answers are correct.

4 Who lived in the land God gave to Abram? (12:6-7)
  1. **Canaanites**
  2. No one
  3. Abram's parents

5 Why did the herdsmen of Abram and Lot quarrel? (13:6-7)
  1. The land could not support both herds.
  2. Abram and Lot had many possessions.
  3. **Both answers are correct.**

6 Why did Abram and Lot go to separate places? (13:8-9)
  1. They did not like each other.
  2. **They did not want anyone to quarrel.**
  3. Lot wanted to return to Haran.

7 Where did Lot choose to live? (13:10-12)
  1. The well-watered plain of the Jordan
  2. Among the cities
  3. **Both answers are correct.**

8 How does the Bible describe the men of Sodom? (13:13)
  1. **They were wicked, and they sinned greatly against the Lord.**
  2. They were relatives of Abram.
  3. Both answers are correct.

9 Where did Abram choose to live? (13:18)
  1. The bank of the Jordan River
  2. **Near the great trees of Mamre in Hebron**
  3. Near the cities

10 What did Abram do after he moved to Hebron? (13:18)
  1. He visited Haran.
  2. **He built an altar to the Lord.**
  3. Both answers are correct.

QUESTIONS FOR ADVANCED COMPETITION

To prepare children for competition, read Genesis 12:1-9; 13:5-18 to them.

1 What did the Lord ask Abram to do? (12:1)
1. To leave his country and his people
2. To leave his father's household
3. To go to the land that the Lord would show him
4. **All of the answers are correct.**

2 Whom did the Lord say that he would make into a great nation? (12:1-2)
1. Lot
2. Noah
3. **Abram**
4. Adam

3 What did the Lord tell Abram at Shechem? (12:6-7)
1. "This is the land of Lot."
2. **"To your offspring I will give this land."**
3. "This is not your land. Continue your travels."
4. "You will fight the Canaanites."

4 Why did the herdsmen of Lot and Abram quarrel? (13:6-7)
1. They were tired of travelling together.
2. Lot's herdsmen stole from Abram's herdsmen.
3. **The land could not support all of them.**
4. They argued about who was best.

5 What was Abram's solution for the quarrelling? (13:8-9)
1. **The two men would go separate ways.**
2. Lot would return to Haran.
3. Only one man would have flocks and herds.
4. All of the answers are correct.

6 To where did Lot and his family move? (13:10-13)
1. The well-watered plain of the Jordan River
2. Near the city of Sodom
3. Near the wicked men
4. **All of the answers are correct.**

7 What did God say about the land that Abram saw? (13:15)
1. Abram could have half of the land.
2. Lot chose the better land.
3. **Abram and his offspring would have all of the land.**
4. All of the answers are correct.

8 To what did God compare Abram's offspring? (13:16)
1. **The dust of the earth**
2. The grains of the sand
3. The hairs on his head
4. The seconds in a day

9 What did God tell Abram to do to the land that God would give to him? (13:17)
1. To build a city
2. To plant an orchard
3. To survey it carefully
4. **To walk through the length and breadth of it**

10 Finish this verse: "By faith Abraham, when called to go to a place he would later receive as his inheritance..." (Hebrews 11:8)
1. **". . . obeyed and went, even though he did not know where he was going."**
2. ". . . decided to go a few years later."
3. ". . . followed his nephew, Lot."
4. ". . . disobeyed and did not follow the Lord."

STUDY 8

Promises and Covenants

Memory Verse

"Do not be afraid, Abram. I am your shield, your very great reward." (Genesis 15:1b)

Biblical Truth

God is worthy of our faith and trust in him.

Teaching Tip

As you lead the Bible study, remind the children that God promised to give Abram a son as an heir.

BIBLICAL COMMENTARY

Abram was a rich and a successful man. However, Abram lacked a son. God told Abram about a great reward, but Abram questioned how great it could be since he was childless. The Lord assured Abram that he would have a son. Abram trusted that God would keep his promise.

Once again, Abram questioned God about this promise. This time, God responded by making a covenant with Abram. Abram arranged the animals in a manner that was common for people who wanted to pledge an oath. Taking this oath was a serious commitment. In this ritual, two people met in the middle of the animal pieces in order to indicate that they both agreed to participate in the oath. In verse 17, God is represented by the firepot and the torch that passed through the pieces. Abram did not pass through the pieces, as he would have done in a normal covenant ceremony. God made the covenant, and Abram received it.

The Lord fulfilled His promise and gave Abram the descendants and the land. Despite Abram's questions, Genesis 15:6 described Abram's faith: "Abram believed the LORD, and he credited it to him as righteousness." As you teach this lesson, help the children to remember that they can trust the promises of God.

WORDS OF OUR FAITH

to be **righteous** -- to be in a right relationship with God and to obey him because of it.

descendants -- the offspring (children, grandchildren, great-grandchildren, etc.) of a person. The descendants of Abram became known as the Israelites.

ACTIVITY

You will need these items for this activity:
- copies of a simple covenant that you will make. You will need one for each child
- pens

Before class, make a simple covenant for each child. Provide a place to put a person's name, the dates, a description of some work to be done, and several lines for signatures. Make enough copies that the children have the opportunity to fill out more than one covenant.

Say, **God called Abram to leave his homeland and travel to an unknown place. God made a covenant with Abram that in the future God would give to him a son. God also promised to give to him all the land that he would show to him. What is a covenant?** (Allow time for the children to answer.) **What was unusual about the covenant that God made with Abram?** (Normally, both people in a covenant would pass through the pieces of animal, but in this covenant only God did that.)

God was faithful to Abram and he guided him on his journey to Canaan. However, God did not complete his promise to Abram until after the covenant was complete.

Pass out copies of the blank contracts to each child. Tell them to think of promises that people make to each other, such as the purchase of an object, or an agreement to do a job for a certain price.

Say, **Today, you will write some covenants. For example: Write a covenant with a friend or parent. Make a promise to do a specific task in your home or at your school for one month. Write your name, the date, and the task that you will do. Then sign your name and ask the other person to sign his or her name.** Instruct the children to give the contract to the other person and to fulfil the promise or covenant for one month. This will remind them of God's promises that he made to us and the promises we make to others.

BIBLICAL LESSON

Prepare a Bible story based on the lesson's scripture verses. Children will understand the lesson better if you tell them the story rather than reading it to them. A simpler version of this story is printed in the back of this book, on pages 122-123. This story is easier to read and understand.

After the story, encourage the children to discuss the story by asking the following questions. This will help them apply it to their lives. There may not be a right or wrong answer.

1. **What situations cause you to doubt God's promises?**
2. **Abram had no children at the time that God promised him descendants as numerous as the stars in the sky. How do you think Abram felt? Would you believe God if you were in Abram's place? Why?**

Say, **How difficult is it to wait for someone to fulfil a promise?** (Allow time for the children to respond.) **God made a covenant with Abram, and God showed Abram how he would fulfil that promise. God would provide an heir to inherit Abram's possessions, and he would give the Promised Land to them.**

Genesis shows that we can trust God. God continues to show us that he is faithful to keep his promises.

MEMORY VERSE

Practice the study's memory verse. You will find suggestions for memory verse activities on pages 110-111.

ADDITIONAL ACTIVITIES

Choose from these options to enhance the children's Bible study.

1. Ask, **To whom does God refer in Genesis 15:13-16? What happened to them?** (This refers to God's people in Egypt. See Exodus 13:14-16.)
2. The Bible uses the words offspring and descendants. These are the children, grandchildren, great-grandchildren, etc. of a person. Write the name of one of the children's grandparents on the board. Then, help the child to write all the descendants.

QUESTIONS FOR BASIC COMPETITION

To prepare the children for competition, read Genesis 15:1-21 to them.

1 Why did Abram think that his servant Eliezer would receive Abram's inheritance? (15:2)

1. Abram was not obedient to the Lord.
2. **Abram did not have a child of his own.**
3. Both answers are correct.

2 Whom did God say would be Abram's heir? (15:4)

1. Eliezer
2. **A son from his own body**
3. No one

3 Why did God take Abram outside? (15:5)

1. To show the heavens and the stars to him
2. To show how many offspring that he would receive
3. **Both answers are correct.**

4 What question did Abram ask the Lord about the land? (15:8)

1. **"How can I know that I will gain possession of it?"**
2. "Why are the Canaanites still in the land?"
3. "When will I have a son to help me?"

5 What did Abram do with the animals that he brought to the Lord? (15:10)

1. **He cut the larger animals in two and arranged the halves opposite each other.**
2. He cut the birds in half.
3. Both answers are correct.

6 When did the thick and dreadful darkness come over Abram? (15:12)

1. As the sun was rising
2. **While Abram was in a deep sleep**
3. Both answers are correct.

7 About whom did the Lord tell Abram? (15:13)

1. **His descendants**
2. His servant, Eliezer
3. Both answers are correct.

8 How long would Abram's descendants live in a country not their own? (15:13)

1. 40 years
2. 100 years
3. **400 years**

9 How would that country treat Abram's descendants? (15:13)

1. **They will be enslaved and mistreated there.**
2. They would be treated well.
3. They would be treated like common people.

10 When did the smoking firepot with a blazing torch appear? (15:17)

1. In the middle of the day
2. **When the sun had set**
3. The morning of the next day

QUESTIONS FOR ADVANCED COMPETITION

To prepare children for competition, read Genesis 15:1-21 to them.

1 What was the word of the Lord that Abram heard in a vision? (15:1)

1. "Do not be afraid."
2. "I am your shield."
3. "I am your very great reward."
4. **All of the answers are correct.**

2 Why did Abram think that his heir would be Eliezer? (15:2)

1. The Lord told Abram that Eliezer would be his heir.
2. **Abram was childless.**
3. Abram had a vision of Eliezer as his heir.
4. Eliezer was Abram's son.

3 Who was Eliezer? (15:2-3)

1. Abram's firstborn son
2. Abram's nephew
3. **A servant in Abram's household**
4. A neighbour's son

4 The Lord told Abram that his offspring would be like what? (15:5)

1. **The stars**
2. Grains of rice
3. The heavens
4. Sand in an hourglass

5 How did Abram respond to the Lord's promise of offspring? (15:6)

1. Abram doubted the Lord.
2. Abram questioned the Lord.
3. **Abram believed the Lord.**
4. Abram rejoiced in the Lord.

6 What would Abram's descendants be in the strange country? (15:13)

1. Strangers
2. Mistreated
3. Slaves
4. **All of the answers are correct.**

7 During Abram's deep sleep, what did the Lord say would happen to Abram? (15:15)

1. He would become a slave.
2. He would never have a child.
3. **He would die in peace at a good old age.**
4. He would never take possession of the land.

8 What appeared when darkness had fallen? (15:17)

1. A rain cloud
2. **A smoking firepot with a blazing torch**
3. An angel
4. Pieces of the animals

9 When did God make the covenant with Abram? (15:12, 17- 18)

1. **The day Abram fell into a deep sleep and the Lord spoke to him about his descendants**
2. The day he arrived in Canaan
3. When Eliezer became his servant
4. All of the answers are correct.

10 Finish this verse: "Do not be afraid, Abram. I am your shield, . . ." (Genesis 15:1b)

1. ". . . and your protector."
2. ". . . who will help you."
3. **". . . your very great reward."**
4. ". . . and your sword."

STUDY 9

Memory Verse

"Because you have done this and have not withheld your son, your only son, I will surely bless you." (Genesis 22:16b-17a)

Biblical Truth

God helps us to obey him in all situations.

Teaching Tip

• God changed Abram's name to Abraham in Genesis 17:5 and told him he would be the father of nations. God changed Sarai's name to Sarah in Genesis 17:15 to signify that she would become a mother of nations. Names had special significance. Help children to understand that when God changed their names, he showed that he had authority over their future. A new name indicates that something significant happened or that it will happen.

• If children ask about circumcision, you might say: **Circumcision has a special religious meaning in the Bible. It was a mark of God's covenant with Abraham, and a physical sign of Abraham's faith and obedience to God's commandments.**

BIBLICAL COMMENTARY

God changed Abram's name in chapter 17 with the confirmation of the covenant. Abram is now Abraham. Chapter 21 tells of the anticipated son, Isaac, who is born to Sarai. Her name becomes Sarah.

The Lord tested Abraham's devotion. He asked Abraham to sacrifice Isaac as an offering of worship to God. Remember, Isaac is not only Abraham's beloved son, but also the means by which God intended to fulfil his promise to Abraham.

Genesis 22:8-12 tells about Abraham's journey which was very emotional for him. Abraham believed that God would provide a sacrifice. Second, Abraham intended to go through with the sacrifice. Finally, the Lord saw Abraham's complete devotion. He did not withhold anything from God, including his son, Isaac.

When God saw Abraham's great faith, he reassured Abraham of the blessings to come. God also promised that he would bless all nations because of Abraham's obedience. Abraham proved that God's faith in him was worthy of the covenant and the blessings he promised.

WORDS OF OUR FAITH

trust -- complete dependence on God and his promises; a belief that God will do what he says

ACTIVITY

You will need these items for this activity:

- a stop watch or clock
- samples of some items that are important to children
- a piece of paper for each child
- pens or pencils

Before class, arrange on a table the items that are important to children. These are items that the children could sacrifice for a week to show their love for God. Provide a large variety of items. These items will represent things that children could sacrifice.

Say, **In today's lesson, God fulfilled his covenant to Abraham when he gave Abraham the promised son. Abraham faithfully trusted God. Have you ever waited for a long time for someone to fulfil a promise?**

God tested Abraham when he asked Abraham to sacrifice his son. Abraham showed his love for God by his willingness to do what God asked.

Point out some of the items on the table. Ask, **Which of these items would be special to you?** (Let the children respond.) **What if God asked you to show him how much you loved him? Would you give up something that was very important to you? What would you do?**

Give each child a piece of paper, and encourage the children to write a poem or draw a picture that reveals how it feels to sacrifice something for God.

BIBLICAL LESSON

Prepare a Bible story based on the lesson's scripture verses. Children will understand the lesson better if you tell them the story rather than reading it to them. A simpler version of this story is printed in the back of this book, on pages 123-124. This story is easier to read and understand.

After the story, encourage the children to discuss the story by asking the following questions. This will help them apply it to their lives. There may not be a right or wrong answer.

1. **What do Abraham's actions tell us about his faith in God?**
2. **What does Abraham's faith teach us about what God wants from us?**
3. **What would be the most difficult thing for you to sacrifice?**

Say, **Abraham waited for many years for a son. After the birth of Isaac, God asked Abraham to sacrifice Isaac.** If the children are concerned about God asking someone to sacrifice a child, tell them that this was a special event. It was the only time God asked someone to do this. **Abraham could not understand what God planned to do, but he obeyed God completely. As a result, God promised to bless Abraham and his family.**

God wants us to have the same kind of faith and the same kind of trust in him.

MEMORY VERSE

Practice the study's memory verse. You will find suggestions for memory verse activities on pages 110-111.

ADDITIONAL ACTIVITIES

Choose from these options to enhance the children's Bible study.

1. Help the children to compare and to contrast the sacrifice Abraham made with the sacrifice God made for us.
2. Write a journal entry for Abraham for the previous day and the day that followed the sacrifice on the mountain.

QUESTIONS FOR BASIC COMPETITION

To prepare the children for competition, read Genesis 21:1-6; 22:1-18 to them.

1 What happened at the very time that God promised? (21:2)

1. **Abraham and Sarah had a son.**
2. The Canaanites left the area.
3. Both answers are correct.

2 What did Abraham and Sarah name their son? (21:4)

1. Abimelech
2. David
3. **Isaac**

3 Where did God ask Abraham to take Isaac? (22:2)

1. To visit Lot
2. **To the region of Moriah**
3. To Haran

4 What did God ask Abraham to do in Moriah? (22:2)

1. **To sacrifice Isaac**
2. To meet with the Canaanites
3. Both answers are correct.

5 Who went with Abraham to Moriah? (22:3)

1. Isaac
2. Two servants
3. **Both answers are correct.**

6 Who asked, "Where is the lamb for the burnt offering?" (22:7)

1. Abraham
2. **Isaac**
3. The servants

7 What happened to Isaac after Abraham built the altar? (22:9)

1. Isaac ran away from Abraham.
2. Isaac sat down, and he refused to move.
3. **Abraham bound Isaac, and he placed Isaac on the altar.**

8 Who stopped Abraham before he sacrificed Isaac? (22:11-12)

1. The servants
2. **The angel of the Lord**
3. Sarah

9 What did the Lord provide for the sacrifice? (22:13)

1. **A ram**
2. A goat
3. A donkey

10 What did the angel of the Lord say about Abraham's willingness to sacrifice his son? (22:16-17)

1. God would bless Abraham.
2. Abraham would have many descendants.
3. **Both answers are correct.**

QUESTIONS FOR ADVANCED COMPETITION

To prepare children for competition, read Genesis 21:1-6; 22:1-18 to them.

1 How did God fulfil his promise to Abraham and Sarah? (21:1-2)

1. Sarah had a child.
2. The child was born at the very time that the Lord promised.
3. The child was born to Abraham in his old age.
4. **All of the answers are correct.**

2 Why did Abraham circumcise Isaac when he was eight days old? (21:3-4)

1. **God commanded it as part of his covenant to Abraham.**
2. Sarah wanted this.
3. Ishmael wanted this.
4. It was a rule of the people of Beersheba.

3 How old was Abraham when Isaac was born? (21:5)

1. **100 years old**
2. 90 years old
3. 99 years old
4. 110 years old

4 After Isaac's birth, what did Sarah say that God had brought to her? (21:6)

1. Sadness
2. Joy
3. **Laughter**
4. Tears

5 Why did Abraham go to the region of Moriah? (22:2)

1. To make a treaty with the Canaanites
2. To move his tents
3. **To sacrifice Isaac**
4. All of the answers are correct.

6 How long did Abraham wait to obey the Lord? (22:3)

1. **He left early the next morning.**
2. He waited a month.
3. He never did what God asked him to do.
4. He waited until the weather was better.

7 Who did Abraham say would provide the lamb for the burnt offering? (22:8)

1. Abraham
2. Isaac
3. The servants
4. **God**

8 What did Abraham do when he reached the place for the sacrifice? (22:9)

1. He raised a tent, and he lived there for a week.
2. **He built an altar, and he placed Isaac on it.**
3. He asked the Lord what to do next.
4. He sacrificed the ram that he brought.

9 Why would Abraham have as many descendants as the stars in the sky? (22:12, 16-18)

1. He did not withhold his only son.
2. He obeyed God.
3. He feared God.
4. **All of the answers are correct.**

10 Finish this verse, "Because you have done this and have not withheld your son, your only son,..." (Genesis 22:16b-17a).

1. **". . . I will surely bless you."**
2. ". . . you will live long in the land I have promised you."
3. ". . . you will be punished."
4. ". . . I will give you another son."

STUDY 10

Here Comes the Bride

Memory Verse

"I will instruct you and teach you in the way you should go; I will counsel you with my loving eye on you." (Psalm 32:8)

Biblical Truth

God cares about our lives and leads us as we follow him.

Teaching Tip

Before you tell the story, ask children to listen for responses from the characters. At the end of the story, ask how many people had to do something in order for Rebekah and Isaac to marry?

BIBLICAL COMMENTARY

God's covenant with Abraham continued through Isaac. It was the highest priority. It was important that Isaac find the right wife to continue God's promise of many descendants for Abraham. This would enable Isaac to fulfil his role in God's covenant.

God's guidance influenced Rebekah and her family. They responded positively to the question, "Will Rebekah go with this man?" Each person had a choice to make. Would they trust God? We do not know the motivation of each person. However, the Bible does indicate that each person was obedient in the steps that led to the marriage of Rebekah and Isaac.

Children learn from this passage that God is concerned with their everyday life, and that God wants to help them make the right choices.

ACTIVITY

Play a game of "Teacher, may I?" To begin the game, the teacher stands at one end of a room while all of the children form a line at the other end. The children take turns and ask "Teacher, may I?" and make a movement suggestion. For example, one child asks, "Teacher, may I take five giant steps forward?" The leader either replies "Yes, you may" or "No, you may not do that, but you may take five small steps instead." The teacher inserts his or her own suggestion. The children usually move closer to the leader but sometimes the teacher's instructions lead the children farther away. Even if the leader makes an unfavourable suggestion, the child must perform it. The first child to reach the leader wins the game.

Some suggestions for movements include:

- Take 3 steps forward. (Use any number.)
- Take 2 steps backward. (Use any number.)
- Take 5 giant steps forward. (This is usually a small number because of the large size of the step.)
- Take 12 baby steps forward. (This is usually a large number because of the small size of the step.)
- Hop forward 5 times like a frog. (Use any number.)
- Run forward while you count to five. (Use any number.)

Play the game again, if time allows.

Say, **In this game, you asked the leader's permission, and you made the choice to follow the leader. You did this even if the leader's will was not your will.**

In today's story, we will learn how several people made choices that were in God's will.

BIBLICAL LESSON

Prepare a Bible story based on the lesson's scripture verses. Children will understand the lesson better if you tell them the story rather than reading it to them. A simpler version of this story is printed in the back of this book, on pages 124-126. This story is easier to read and understand.

After the story, encourage the children to discuss the story by asking the following questions. This will help them apply it to their lives. There may not be a right or wrong answer.

1. **Have you ever waited a long time to get something that you wanted? Was it worth the wait?**
2. **Why was it important for God to provide a wife for Isaac?**
3. **Who made a good choice in this story and what was the choice?** (There could be more than one good answer.)
4. **How does the memory verse, Psalm 32:8, relate to this story?**

Say, **God cared about Abraham, Isaac and Rebekah. God also cares about your life. You can ask God to help you make right choices. One of the things that you learned in Genesis is that God is faithful and that God keeps his promises. God knows you, and he knows your needs. When you make a choice, you can ask God to help you make the right choice.**

MEMORY VERSE

Practice the study's memory verse. You will find suggestions for memory verse activities on pages 110-111.

ADDITIONAL ACTIVITIES

Choose from these options to enhance the children's Bible study.

1. Say, **Pretend that you are Rebekah. Write a diary entry that tells how you felt when you met the servant and he gave you those expensive gifts. How would you feel about going to a different land to marry a stranger? Pretend you are the servant. What were your thoughts and reactions?**

2. Research Old Testament wedding customs or talk about how wedding customs changed in your country.

3. Compare a wedding today in your town with the wedding of Rebekah. How are they alike? How are they different?

QUESTIONS FOR BASIC COMPETITION

To prepare the children for competition, read Genesis 24:1-4, 10-21, 28-33, 50-54, 61-67 to them.

1 Why did Abraham send his chief servant to his relatives? (24:4)

1. To bring back his father to him
2. **To find a wife for his son, Isaac**
3. To worship in his homeland

2 For what did the servant pray when he reached the well at Nahor? (24:11-12)

1. **Success**
2. Rest for the camels
3. Both answers are correct.

3 Why did the servant ask Rebekah for some water? (24:13-14)

1. **He wanted to determine if she was the woman whom God chose for Isaac.**
2. She was the only one who spoke his language.
3. She was the only one at the well.

4 Why did Laban hurry out to the well to meet the servant? (24:28-31)

1. Rebekah ran home, and she told her family what happened.
2. Laban prepared the house for him and a place for his camels.
3. **Both answers are correct.**

5 What did Laban and Bethuel say after the servant explained why he came? (24:50)

1. **"This is from the LORD."**
2. "We will not let Rebekah go with you."
3. Both answers are correct.

6 What did the servant give Rebekah and her family? (24:53)

1. Gold and silver jewellery
2. Clothing and costly gifts
3. **Both answers are correct.**

7 When did Rebekah leave with the servant? (24:54)

1. A week later
2. **The next morning**
3. Ten days later

8 Where was Isaac when Rebekah saw him? (24:63-64)

1. **In the field, meditating**
2. In his tent, eating
3. By the river, fishing

9 What did the servant do when he saw Isaac? (24:66)

1. He prayed to God.
2. **He told Isaac everything that he did.**
3. Both answers are correct.

10 How did Isaac feel after he married Rebekah? (24:67)

1. He loved Rebekah.
2. She comforted him after his mother's death.
3. **Both answers are correct.**

QUESTIONS FOR ADVANCED COMPETITION

To prepare children for competition, read Genesis 24:1-4, 10-21, 28-33, 50-54, 61-67 to them.

1 How had the Lord blessed Abraham? (24:1)
   1. With much money
   2. In every way
   3. In most ways
   4. With everything he wanted

2 Why was it important where the servant found a wife for Isaac? (24:3-4)
   1. Isaac wanted to marry a Canaanite, and Abraham did not want that to happen.
   2. Isaac did not understand the language of the Canaanites.
   3. Abraham wanted a wife for Isaac from his own country, not from the Canaanites.
   4. It was not important. The servant could choose from any place.

3 Why did the servant pray at the well of Nahor? (24:12)
   1. The first girl that he found was not the right one.
   2. He needed to ask the Lord to give him success to find a wife for Isaac.
   3. He felt discouraged, and he was ready to go home.
   4. All of the answers are correct.

4 How did the servant know that his journey was successful? (24:14, 18-19)
   1. Rebekah told him that an angel sent her to the well.
   2. Rebekah gave some water to him and to his camels, as he had prayed.
   3. God sent him a vision of what she looked like.
   4. All of the answers are correct.

5 What happened at Rebekah and Laban's house? (24:32-33)
   1. The servants brought some water to wash their feet.
   2. The servants gave some straw and fodder to the camels.
   3. The servant told them why he was there.
   4. All of the answers are correct.

6 According to Laban and Bethuel, who directed the servant's meeting with Rebekah? (24:50)
   1. Isaac
   2. Abraham
   3. The Lord
   4. Rebekah

7 What did Abraham's servant do when he heard what Laban and Bethuel said? (24:52)
   1. He bowed down to the ground before the Lord.
   2. He offered a sacrifice to the Lord.
   3. He celebrated with a great feast.
   4. He boasted of his great accomplishment.

8 What happened after Rebekah saw Isaac? (24:65-67)
   1. She covered herself with her veil.
   2. The servant told Isaac about everything that happened.
   3. Isaac married Rebekah.
   4. All of the answers are correct.

9 When did Rebekah comfort Isaac? (24:67)
   1. After his mother's death
   2. When he saw Rebekah on the camel
   3. After the birth of their first son
   4. When she agreed to go with the servant

10 Finish this verse: "I will instruct you and teach you in the way you should go; I will counsel you . . ." (Psalm 32:8).
   1. ". . . and keep you."
   2. ". . . and give you wisdom."
   3. ". . . with my loving eye on you."
   4. ". . . and provide for you."

STUDY 11

Memory Verse
"Even small children are known by their actions, so is their conduct really pure and up right?"
(Proverbs 20:11)

Biblical Truth
God works in our lives, even when we encounter conflict.

Teaching Tip
As you lead the Bible study, emphasize that although Jacob and Esau both did things that were wrong, God was still faithful to keep his covenant.

BIBLICAL COMMENTARY

Chapter 25, and the chapters that follow it, develop two major themes. The first is how one generation passed the covenant to the next. The second is the struggle between two brothers. After Abraham died, God blessed Isaac who became the next generation's heir. Esau was the next in line to become the heir to the family and God's covenant. Because of the shrewdness of Jacob, Esau flippantly sold his future for a lunch (25:34).

Family dynamics and relationships are the major themes of this study. This family encounters death, births, deceit, favouritism, power struggles, broken relationships, and hints of marital discord. As we follow this family's story, sometimes God will appear in the forefront, and, at other times, in the background. But, he worked with this family, even though at times they were dysfunctional.

WORDS OF OUR FAITH

a **promise** -- a statement that someone will do something. In the Bible, God made promises. He always kept his promises.

an **oath** -- a strong promise where someone asks God to witness the oath and to judge a person if her or she breaks it.

the **birthright** -- the privilege that belongs to the firstborn son of a family. It meant the eldest son received influence and a double portion of inheritance after his father's death. The eldest son would be the next leader of the family.

ACTIVITY

You will need these items for this activity:

- a sheet of paper
- a bowl
- a spoon

Before class, cut the paper into five pieces. Cut each piece of paper into a unique shape to represent a piece of meat. Write one of the questions below on each shape. Do not write the answers. You may write additional questions. Hide the pieces of paper around the room.

1. Did Esau and Jacob often compete with each other? (Yes, even before they were born)
2. Who became Isaac's favourite son? (Esau)
3. Who became Rebekah's favourite son? (Jacob)
4. What are some issues that cause brothers or sisters to fight? (Allow time for the children to respond.)
5. How did Jacob trick Esau? (He convinced Esau to sell his birthright for some stew.)

Say, **In the room are some pieces of paper that have the shape of a piece of meat. Each one has a question on it. Find these pieces of paper, and place them in this bowl.**

After the children find the pieces of paper, select a volunteer to stir the bowl with the spoon. Let a volunteer choose one question to answer. Repeat this with all the questions. If the children are unfamiliar with this story, complete this activity after you read the Bible story. You may combine the activity questions with the questions in the next section.

BIBLICAL LESSON

Prepare a Bible story based on the lesson's scripture verses. Children will understand the lesson better if you tell them the story rather than reading it to them. A simpler version of this story is printed in the back of this book, on pages 126-127. This story is easier to read and understand.

After the story, encourage the children to discuss the story by asking the following questions. This will help them apply it to their lives. There may not be a right or wrong answer.

1. **In your opinion, what was it like for Jacob to know that Esau was Isaac's favourite?**
2. **In your opinion, what was it like for Esau to know that Jacob was Rebekah's favourite?**
3. **What are some characteristics of Jacob?**
4. **How do you feel when your brother, sister, or friend cheats you?**

Say, **God kept his promise to Isaac. He blessed Rebekah with two sons instead of** one. However, the two sons fought and competed with each other. Jacob even took advantage of his older brother so that he could obtain the birthright. Esau sold his birthright for a bowl of stew.

This story happened in Old Testament times. However, family problems still happen today. God is still faithful, even when members of a family struggle. God always keeps his promise to be with us and help us in difficult situations.

MEMORY VERSE

Practice the study's memory verse. You will find suggestions for memory verse activities on pages 110-111.

ADDITIONAL ACTIVITIES

Choose from these options to enhance the children's Bible study.

1. Select two volunteers from the class. Have the first volunteer portray Esau. Have the second volunteer portray Jacob. Tell the children to dramatize the sale of Esau's birthright to Jacob.
2. Allow the children to share ways that God helped their family. Make a list of these stories. Use this list to show the children that God keeps his promises today.

QUESTIONS FOR BASIC COMPETITION

To prepare the children for competition, read Genesis 25:5-11, 19-34 to them.

1 What happened when Abraham died? (25:8-10)

1. Isaac moved to the land of Rebekah's family.
2. **Ishmael and Isaac buried Abraham with Sarah.**
3. Both answers are correct.

2 Why did Isaac pray to the Lord for Rebekah? (25:21)

1. **She could not have children.**
2. She wanted to see her family.
3. Both answers are correct.

3 What did the Lord tell Rebekah about her babies? (25:23)

1. They would live separate lives.
2. The older would serve the younger.
3. **Both answers are correct.**

4 What were the names of Rebekah's twin boys? (25:24-26)

1. Isaac and Laban
2. Isaac and Esau
3. **Esau and Jacob**

5 Which of these statements is true of Esau? (25:27)

1. He was a farmer who liked the fields.
2. **He was a skilful hunter who liked the open country.**
3. He was quiet and liked to stay among the tents.

6 Which of these statements is true of Jacob? (25:27)

1. **He was quiet, and he liked to stay among the tents.**
2. He was a fisherman who liked the river.
3. He was a skilful hunter who liked the open country.

7 When did Jacob say to Esau, "First, sell me your birthright"? (25:29-31)

1. After Esau came home famished
2. After Esau asked Jacob for some stew
3. **Both answers are correct.**

8 Why did Esau say he was about to die? (25:30, 32)

1. He was wounded.
2. **He was hungry.**
3. He was sick.

9 How did Esau sell his birthright to Jacob? (25:33)

1. **He swore an oath.**
2. He signed a paper.
3. He made a pile of stones.

10 What did Esau despise? (25:34)

1. The life of a hunter
2. The food he ate
3. **His birthright**

QUESTIONS FOR ADVANCED COMPETITION

To prepare children for competition, read Genesis 25:5-11, 19-34 to them.

1 What happened when Abraham died? (25:5-11)

1. Ishmael and Isaac buried him.
2. His sons buried him with Sarah.
3. God blessed Isaac.
4. **All of the answers are correct.**

2 Whom did Isaac marry? (25:20)

1. Hagar
2. Sarah
3. **Rebekah**
4. Keturah

3 For how many years were Isaac and Rebekah married when she had twin boys? (25:20, 26)

1. 10 years
2. **20 years**
3. 2 years
4. 5 years

4 What did the Lord say about the two nations in Rebekah's womb? (25:23)

1. The younger would serve the older.
2. They would always be together.
3. **The older would serve the younger.**
4. All of the answers are correct.

5 Why did Isaac and Rebekah name their older son Esau? (25:25)

1. He was a skilful hunter.
2. **He had a red complexion and much hair on his body.**
3. He liked the open country.
4. He was hungry.

6 How did Isaac and Rebekah feel about their sons? (25:28)

1. They loved both of their sons equally.
2. They both preferred Jacob.
3. Isaac preferred Jacob. Rebekah preferred Esau.
4. **Isaac preferred Esau. Rebekah preferred Jacob.**

7 How were Esau and Jacob different from each other? (25:27-28)

1. **Esau liked the open country, and Jacob liked to stay among the tents.**
2. Esau liked cooking, and Jacob liked hunting.
3. Esau was a quiet man, and Jacob was a skilful hunter.
4. All of the answers are correct.

8 Why did Esau sell his birthright to Jacob? (25:30-33)

1. Esau did not understand that he sold it.
2. **He was hungry**
3. Jacob promised to give the birthright back.
4. The Bible doesn't say.

9 What did Esau despise? (25:34)

1. His mother
2. His father
3. **His birthright**
4. The stew that his brother gave him

10 Finish this verse: "Even small children are known by their actions, so is..." (Proverbs 20:11)

1. "...he obeys or he disobeys his parents."
2. **"...their conduct really pure and upright?"**
3. "...he follows God or he does not."
4. "...he fights with others or he does not fight with others."

STUDY 12

Deceived!

"Whoever of you loves life and desires to see many good days, keep your tongue from evil and your lips from telling lies." (Psalm 34:12-13)

Biblical Truth
God allows us to make choices.

Teaching Tip
Teach the children that God allows us to make choices. Sometimes, people make choices that harm others. Even though people sometimes make the wrong choice, God gives us the freedom to choose between what is right and what is wrong. Our choices bring consequences. Good choices bring good consequences. Bad choices bring bad consequences.

BIBLICAL COMMENTARY

What happened to Isaac's family? They had a lot of problems. There were disagreements with neighbors about wells. Isaac lied to the king of the Philistines and said that Rebekah was his sister, not his wife. Esau married two Hittite women who were "a source of grief to Isaac and Rebekah." The family was deceitful and selfish. Rebekah took advantage of Isaac's blindness to advance Jacob instead of Esau.

The way that Jacob received his blessing was another deception. Jacob gained material possessions through the birthright of Esau. Jacob then gained the spiritual blessings of God through the blessing of Isaac.

Abraham's family had many problems that involved betrayal between husband and wife and between brothers. The betrayal resulted in Esau's plot to murder Jacob. Isaac and Rebekah sent Jacob to the homeland of Rebekah. This separated the family.

In this passage, there are many examples of people who made wrong choices. God did not intervene in Jacob's deception of Esau. However, God is not weak and people cannot manipulate him. God chooses to give us freedom to make choices, and he allows us to suffer the consequences. In future studies, the children will learn how God worked with Jacob to achieve God's purposes.

WORDS OF OUR FAITH

free will -- the ability and the freedom to make choices. God gives free will to everyone.

the **blessing** -- a covenant that God established between himself and Abraham. Abraham passed it to Isaac, who was the recognized heir of Abraham. Jacob deceived his father and brother. As a result, Isaac passed the blessing to Jacob.

ACTIVITY

You will need these items for this activity:

- a piece of cloth for a blindfold

Choose one of the children as a volunteer. Ask him or her to sit in the middle of the classroom. Place the blindfold over the child's eyes.

Say, **Isaac was blind. Rebekah and Jacob took advantage of the blindness of Isaac. Today, our volunteer will try to recognize people without the use of his or her eyes.**

Tell one of the children to sit across from the child with the blindfold. The child with the blindfold child may feel the arms or the face of the child. Then, ask the child with the blindfold to guess who the other child is. Repeat this with all of the other students. Use a pencil and paper to record the number of guesses that the child makes.

Say, **We are often unable to tell if a** choice is right or wrong. Even when we have evidence, we may still make the wrong choice.

Say, **We will repeat this activity. Now we will do it differently. If the child with the blindfold is unable to decide who is in front of him or her after two guesses, the child may ask one person. That person will tell who is in front of the guesser.**

Choose a child to give the answers to the child with the blindfold. Repeat the activity, but use only two children this time. Place a child in front of the child with the blindfold. Let the child make two guesses orally. If the guesses are wrong, let the designated child tell who the child is.

Say, **When we have difficult choices to make, we need help. It is important to ask God for help with these choices. He will help us when we ask him.**

BIBLICAL LESSON

Prepare a Bible story based on the lesson's scripture verses. Children will understand the lesson better if you tell them the story rather than reading it to them. A simpler version of this story is printed in the back of this book, on pages 127-128. This story is easier to read and understand.

After the story, encourage the children to discuss the story by asking the following questions. This will help them apply it to their lives. There may not be a right or wrong answer.

1. **Rebekah planned for Jacob to steal Esau's blessing. Why did Jacob**

agree to participate?

2. Sometimes, our friends encourage us to do things that are wrong. What do you say to your friends when this happens?

3. Jacob deceived Isaac. Has anyone deceived you? How did you feel?

4. Esau wanted to kill Jacob for what Jacob did. When someone does something wrong to you, how do you react? Is it easy to forgive others? Where do you find the strength to forgive?

Say, **We have studied an amazing Bible story. It had elements of trickery and deceit. We have learned that God allows us to make choices. Those choices affect our future. Jacob made a bad choice that had a permanent effect. However, God stayed faithful to his covenant.**

Today, God allows us to make choices. These choices will affect our futures.

MEMORY VERSE

Practice the study's memory verse. You will find suggestions for memory verse activities on pages 110-111.

ADDITIONAL ACTIVITIES

Choose from these options to enhance the children's Bible study.

1. As a class, make a list of choices that the children will face. These choices may be temptations they experience at home, at school, or with their friends. For each choice, discuss what the future consequences may be for each decision.

2. Say, **Jacob chose to participate in Rebekah's plan to deceive Isaac. Imagine that Jacob decided not to participate. What are some possible consequences of this decision? What would be different in this story?**

QUESTIONS FOR BASIC COMPETITION

To prepare the children for competition, read Genesis 25:5-11, 19-34 to them.

1 What did Isaac ask Esau to do? (27:3-4)
1. To dig a new well
2. To ask Jacob to bring him a goat
3. **To hunt some wild game and to prepare a meal for him**

2 What did Isaac want to give Esau? (27:6-7)
1. Some food
2. **His blessing**
3. New clothes

3 What did Rebekah do after she overheard the words of Esau and Isaac? (27:8-10)
1. **She told Jacob to serve Isaac a meal.**
2. She helped Esau prepare the food that he brought.
3. Both answers are correct.

4 How did Rebekah and Jacob trick Isaac? (27:15-17)
1. They made Isaac think that Jacob was Esau.
2. They served Isaac the meal while Esau hunted wild animals.
3. **Both of the answers are correct.**

5 What did Isaac say when he touched Jacob? (27:22)
1. "The voice is the voice of Esau."
2. **"The voice is the voice of Jacob."**
3. "The hands are the hands of Jacob."

6 What happened when Esau returned from his hunt? (27:30-31)
1. **He also prepared a meal to serve to Isaac.**
2. Jacob blessed Esau.
3. Both answers are correct.

7 Why did Isaac tremble violently? (27:33, 35-36)
1. **He realized he had blessed Jacob.**
2. The food made him sick.
3. He lost his ability to see.

8 How did Jacob deceive Esau? (27:36)
1. He took Esau's birthright.
2. He took Esau's blessing.
3. **Both answers are correct.**

9 Where did Isaac say that Esau would dwell? (27:39)
1. Away from the earth's richness
2. Away from the dew of heaven above
3. **Both answers are correct**

10 When did Esau plan to kill Jacob? (27:41)
1. The next morning
2. When Jacob forgot what he did
3. **After Isaac died**

QUESTIONS FOR ADVANCED COMPETITION

To prepare children for competition, read Genesis 27:1-41 to them.

1 Why did Isaac send Esau to the open country? (27:3)

1. To tend to the goats
2. **To hunt some wild game**
3. To find a place to live
4. To bless Jacob while Esau was absent

2 What instructions did Isaac give to Esau? (27:2-4)

1. "Get your weapons."
2. "Hunt some wild game for me."
3. "Prepare me the kind of tasty food I like."
4. **All of the answers are correct.**

3 What did Isaac plan to give to Esau? (27:4)

1. A meal
2. **His blessing**
3. A gift of land
4. 100 goats

4 What did Jacob say when Rebekah requested that Jacob serve the meal to Isaac? (27:12)

1. "I will not deceive my father."
2. **"I would appear to trick him."**
3. "Mother, this is a deceitful plan."
4. "Esau will be left with nothing."

5 When Jacob feared that Isaac would curse him, what did Rebekah say? (27:13)

1. **"Let the curse fall on me."**
2. "Your father will not curse you."
3. "Your father will curse Esau."
4. She said nothing.

6 How did Rebekah and Jacob deceive Isaac? (27:14-17)

1. Rebekah made a meal for Isaac.
2. Jacob wore goatskins and the clothes of Esau.
3. Jacob served the meal that Rebekah made.
4. **All of the answers are correct.**

7 What did Isaac do when he smelled Esau's clothes on Jacob? (27:27)

1. He placed a curse on Jacob.
2. **He blessed Jacob.**
3. He told Esau what Jacob did.
4. He called for Esau.

8 What did Esau do when he came back from hunting? (27:30-31)

1. He asked Jacob to cook the food.
2. He told Isaac that he and Jacob should share the blessing.
3. **He prepared the food, and he brought it to his father.**
4. All of the answers are correct.

9 What happened when Isaac and Esau realized what Jacob did? (27:33-34, 41)

1. Isaac trembled violently.
2. Esau burst out with a loud and bitter cry.
3. Esau planned to kill Jacob.
4. **All of the answers are correct.**

10 Finish this verse: "Whoever of you loves life and desires to see many good days, keep your tongue from evil..." (Psalm 34:12-13)

1. **"...and your lips from telling lies."**
2. "...and your mind from sin."
3. "...and your family from harm."
4. "...and your hands from wrong."

STUDY 13

A Fresh Start

Memory Verse

"I am the God of your father Abraham. Do not be afraid, for I am with you." (Genesis 26:24b)

Biblical Truth

God works in our lives, even when we encounter conflict.

Teaching Tip

As you lead the Bible study, focus on the ways God spoke to Jacob. Point out to the children that Laban deceived Jacob, who deceived his father and brother. Tell the children that wrong actions always have consequences.

BIBLICAL COMMENTARY

Rebekah told Jacob to flee from Esau. Jacob went to Haran, his mother's homeland, to live with Laban, the brother of Rebekah.

While Jacob travelled, he encountered the Lord. The Lord confirmed that he would bless him, even though Jacob deceived his brother to get the blessing. This was the same blessing that God gave to Abraham and to Isaac.

Jacob safely arrived at his destination, and Laban welcomed him. At first, the relationship between Laban and Jacob was good. Jacob exchanged his work for the privilege of marrying Rachel, the daughter of Laban.

Like Jacob, Laban was someone who deceived others. Laban secretly substituted Leah for Rachel as the bride. Jacob agreed to work seven more years for Rachel.

In spite of Jacob's failures, God honoured his covenant to Jacob. This study shows God's ability to accomplish his purposes, despite the choices of people.

WORDS OF OUR FAITH

choices -- what we decide to do in a situation. We make right choices when we obey God. We make wrong choices when we disobey God.

worship -- honour, reverence, or adoration for God. When we worship God, we declare that God is the ruler of our lives.

descendants -- children who are born to a person or his children.

ACTIVITY

You will need these items for this activity:

- a large stone
- several small pieces of paper
- some markers, pencils, or crayons
- some tape

Before class, place the stone in the middle of the room. If possible, place it in an upright position.

Say, **Jacob placed a stone in Bethel as a reminder of his conversation with God. In the conversation, God told Jacob that he will watch over Jacob wherever he went.**

God watches over us too. Think about a time when you needed something and God provided it for you or your family. Write briefly on a piece of paper what God provided. We will attach these papers to our stone and say "Thank you" to God.

After the children have attached their papers, let volunteers share what they wrote. Say, **This stone is a reminder of all of the things that God provided for us. God is faithful to us even though we sometimes disappoint him. He provides for us, and he speaks to us. We will learn more about a special time when God spoke to Jacob.**

BIBLICAL LESSON

Prepare a Bible story based on the lesson's scripture verses. Children will understand the lesson better if you tell them the story rather than reading it to them. A simpler version of this story is printed in the back of this book, on pages 129-130. This story is easier to read and understand.

After the story, encourage the children to discuss the story by asking the following questions. This will help them apply it to their lives. There may not be a right or wrong answer.

1. **A monument helps us to remember something or someone who is important. Jacob used a stone as a monument to remember God's provision for him. What are some other ways we can remember how God provided for us?**

2. **How did Jacob feel when Laban deceived him? How could the deception of Laban make Jacob feel about the way he treated Esau?**

3. **God spoke to Jacob by using a dream. How does God speak to people today? How can we learn to listen to God?**

Say, **God used a dream to communicate with Jacob. In the dream, God told Jacob that all of God's promises would happen. Jacob promised God that he would worship him, and he would give one-tenth of everything he owned to God.**

How does God send messages to us today? He may use a voice within us,

the Bible, a song, a lesson, a sermon, or friendships with other Christians. There are other ways that God can speak to us. We must learn to listen to what God wants to tell us.

MEMORY VERSE

Practice the study's memory verse. You will find suggestions for memory verse activities on pages 110-111.

ADDITIONAL ACTIVITIES

Choose from these options to enhance the children's Bible study.

1. Say, **Jacob saw a ladder that led from earth to heaven. What do you think this ladder looked like? As a class, draw a picture of the ladder. Ask for suggestions from the class.**

2. Say, **Jacob worked for Laban for 14 years, so that he could marry Rachel. Was this a wise thing for him to do? Why? Think of something you want very much. Are you willing to work hard to obtain it? Why?**

QUESTIONS FOR BASIC COMPETITION

To prepare the children for competition, read Genesis 28:10-22; 29:14b-30 to them.

1 Where did Jacob see the stairway? (28:10-12)
1. On the way to Haran
2. In his dream
3. **Both answers are correct.**

2 Who spoke to Jacob in his dream? (28:12-13)
1. Rebekah
2. **The Lord**
3. Esau

3 Whom did God say would be like the dust of the earth? (28:14)
1. **Jacob's descendants**
2. Jacob's enemies
3. Jacob's friends

4 What did Jacob do after he awoke? (28:20)
1. He turned around and went home.
2. **He made a vow to God.**
3. Both answers are correct.

5 What did Jacob ask God to do? (28:20)
1. To be with him and to watch over him
2. To give him food to eat and clothes to wear
3. **Both answers are correct.**

6 With whom did Jacob stay in Haran? (29:14)
1. Esau
2. **Laban**
3. Rebekah

7 Whom did Jacob want to marry? (29:18)
1. **Rachel**
2. Leah
3. Zilpah

8 Whom did Laban give first to Jacob to marry? (29:23)
1. Bilhah
2. Rachel
3. **Leah**

9 For how many more years did Jacob work for Rachel? (29:27)
1. **7 more years**
2. 2 more years
3. 5 more years

10 Whom did Jacob love more? (29:30)
1. Leah
2. **Rachel**
3. Bilhah

QUESTIONS FOR ADVANCED COMPETITION

To prepare children for competition, read Genesis 28:10-22; 29:14b-30 to them.

1 What happened to Jacob on the way to Haran? (28:10-13)

1. He became sick.
2. Esau chased him into the desert.
3. **The Lord appeared to him in a dream.**
4. Rebekah went with Jacob to Haran.

2 What did Jacob see in his dream? (28:12-13)

1. A stairway resting on the earth
2. Angels ascending and descending on the stairway
3. The Lord standing above the stairway
4. **All of the answers are correct.**

3 What did the Lord say that he would do for Jacob? (28:15)

1. Never allow harm to come to him
2. **Watch over him wherever he went**
3. Kill all his enemies
4. Give him two wives

4 What did Jacob say about his dream?(28:16-17)

1. "Surely the LORD is in this place."
2. "How awesome is this place!"
3. "This is the gate of heaven."
4. **All of the answers are correct.**

5 What did Jacob name the place where the Lord spoke to him in a dream? (28:19)

1. **Bethel**
2. Luz
3. Haran
4. Beersheba

6 Whom did Jacob intend to marry? (29:20)

1. Bilhah
2. Leah
3. **Rachel**
4. Zilpah

7 Whom did Laban give to Leah as a maidservant? (29:24)

1. Rachel
2. Bilhah
3. Rebekah
4. **Zilpah**

8 How did Laban deceive Jacob? (29:23, 25)

1. He did not pay Jacob.
2. **He gave Leah to Jacob instead of Rachel.**
3. He told Esau where Jacob was.
4. All of the answers are correct.

9 How long did Jacob work before he married Rachel? (29:20, 27)

1. 7 years
2. 21 years
3. 7 months
4. **14 years**

10 Finish this verse: "I am the God of your father Abraham. Do not be afraid..." (Genesis 26:24b)

1. **"...for I am with you."**
2. "...for I am not angry with you."
3. "...for I will never forsake you."
4. "...for I will leave soon."

STUDY 14

Danger and the Dreamer

Memory Verse

"The LORD is close to the brokenhearted and saves those who are crushed in spirit. A righteous person may have many troubles, but the LORD delivers him from them all."
(Psalm 34:18-19)

Biblical Truth

God allows people to make choices, and people are responsible for those choices.

Teaching Tip

• As you lead the Bible study, remind the children of the things that Jacob did. Even though Jacob's choices caused much pain to his family, God still worked in their lives.

• God changed Jacob's name to Israel in Genesis 35:10. Remind children that names were meaningful. After he struggled with God, Jacob was a changed man.

BIBLICAL COMMENTARY

In Studies 12 and 13, we learned about the deceit of Jacob. In this study, we will learn about the negative consequences of his actions.

Genesis 29—37 tells about the life of Jacob: his tense relationship with Laban, his wealth, and his reunion with Esau. He married two sisters, and he fathered eleven sons by four women. After their struggle, the Lord changed Jacob's name to Israel.

Jacob made many mistakes. He cheated Esau (27:36), and Laban cheated him (29:25). Jacob lied to Isaac (27:19), and Jacob believed a lie that his sons told him (37:32).

Jacob's marriages to Rachel and Leah caused the tension between the siblings. Jacob loved Rachel more than Leah. Jacob's favouritism of Joseph made his other sons angry. God honoured his promise to Jacob, but Jacob was not as faithful as his grandfather, Abraham.

Help the children to understand that sibling rivalry and deception have negative effects. Negative consequences of bad choices cannot be altered, but people can learn from their mistakes and the mistakes of others.

WORDS OF OUR FAITH

to **mourn** -- to show sadness, usually when someone dies. It also means to feel great sorrow for personal sins and for all the sin and evil in the world.

73

the twelve tribes of Israel -- The 12 sons of Israel (Jacob) were the ancestors for the people of Israel: Reuben, Simeon, Levi, Judah, Dan, Naphtali, Gad, Asher, Issachar, Zebulun, Joseph and Benjamin. Levi's tribe was special, and served God's temple. Joseph's descendants were divided into the two tribes of his sons, Ephraim and Manasseh.

a **cistern** -- a deep pit for storing water.

a **shekel** -- a unit of weight, approximately 10 grams. Joseph's brother sold him into slavery for 20 shekels of silver.

ACTIVITY

You will need these items for this activity:
- a small table
- two chairs

Before class, set the table in the middle of the room, with the two chairs on opposite sides.

Divide the class into two teams. Say, **Now, we will play a game. Each team will send one person to the table. Place both of your hands on the table. I will ask a question. If you know the answer, raise your hand. The first person who raises his or her hand may answer the question. If the answer is correct, then that team gets a point.**

Then two new players will sit at the table, and they will receive a new question. We will play until we answer all of the questions. At the end of the game, the team with the highest score wins!

Use the following questions. You may create more questions if you need them.

1. **What would it be like to have many brothers who hate you?** (Accept any reasonable answer.)
2. **Why did Joseph's brothers hate him?** (He was their father's favourite son.)
3. **What did Joseph's dreams mean?** (One day Joseph would rule over his father and brothers.)
4. **What did Joseph's brothers do to him?** (They sold him to Ishmaelite or Midianite merchants who took him to Egypt.)
5. **How did Jacob's sons deceive him?** (They made him believe that an animal killed Joseph.)

BIBLICAL LESSON

Prepare a Bible story based on the lesson's scripture verses. Children will understand the lesson better if you tell them the story rather than reading it to them. A simpler version of this story is printed in the back of this book, on pages 130-132. This story is easier to read and understand.

After the story, encourage the children to discuss the story by asking the following questions. This will help them apply it to their lives. There may not be a right or wrong answer.

1. **Why were Joseph's brothers jealous of him? Have you ever felt jealous of one of your friends? How did you act toward that person?**
2. **How did Joseph feel about his**

dreams? Did Joseph boast to his brothers? Have you ever boasted to someone? Do you like to hear someone boast?

3. Joseph's brothers mistreated Joseph. Have you been mistreated by your family or friends? How did you respond?

4. Jacob was very sad when he thought Joseph was dead. How did you feel when you lost something or someone who is precious to you?

Say, **Jacob deceived Esau and disobeyed God. Joseph's brothers did evil against Joseph. Then, Joseph's brothers deceived Jacob.**

God allows us the freedom to make choices. However, our choices affect us and others. What you say and do today may affect you as an adult. Those choices may also affect your children.

MEMORY VERSE

Practice the study's memory verse. You will find suggestions for memory verse activities on pages 110-111.

ADDITIONAL ACTIVITIES

Choose from these options to enhance the children's Bible study.

1. Ask the children to use crayons or markers and paper to illustrate Joseph's dreams. Let the children show these illustrations to the class.

2. Say, **Imagine that the brothers decided not to sell Joseph to the merchants. How would Joseph react to his brothers after he came out of the cistern?**

3. Use strips of coloured paper to recreate Joseph's ornamented robe. Tape the strips of paper to the wall to create a picture of the robe.

QUESTIONS FOR BASIC COMPETITION

To prepare the children for competition, read Genesis 37:1-36 to them.

1 Why did Joseph's brothers hate him? (37:3-4)
1. Jacob loved Joseph more than he loved his other sons.
2. Joseph was born to Jacob in his old age
3. **Both answers are correct.**

2 What caused Joseph's brothers to hate him even more? (37:5-8)
1. **Joseph told them about his dream.**
2. Joseph never worked with them.
3. They hated him without a reason.

3 Why did Joseph go to Shechem? (37:13-14)
1. To check on his brothers
2. To bring back word about his brothers to Jacob
3. **Both answers are correct.**

4 What did the brothers want to do to Joseph? (37:19-20)
1. To leave him with all the flocks
2. **To kill him and throw him into a cistern**
3. To send him home to his father

5 Who tried to rescue Joseph? (37:21-22)
1. The Lord
2. Jacob
3. **Reuben**

6 What did Joseph's brothers take from him? (37:23)
1. His staff
2. **His robe**
3. His sandals

7 Who came while Joseph's brothers ate their meal? (37:25)
1. **A caravan of Ishmaelites**
2. Judah
3. Jacob

8 Where was the caravan going? (37:25)
1. To Dothan
2. **To Egypt**
3. To Shechem

9 What did the brothers do when the Ishmaelite merchants came? (37:28)
1. They pulled Joseph out of the cistern.
2. They sold Joseph for 20 shekels of silver.
3. **Both answers are correct.**

10 What happened when Joseph's brothers showed the robe to Jacob? (37:34-35)
1. **Jacob mourned for Joseph and would not be comforted.**
2. Jacob asked if they lied.
3. Both answers are correct.

QUESTIONS FOR ADVANCED COMPETITION

To prepare children for competition, read Genesis 37:1-36 to them.

1 Where did Jacob live? (37:1)
1. Shechem
2. Haran
3. Bethel
4. **Canaan**

2 Why was Joseph the favourite son of Jacob? (37:3)
1. He was Leah's son.
2. **Jacob was old when Joseph was born.**
3. He was the son that God promised to give to Jacob.
4. All of the answers are correct.

3 What did Joseph do to make his brothers jealous and hate him? (37:5-11)
1. He lied about his dreams.
2. He became the wealthiest son.
3. **He told about a dream in which their sheaves of corn bowed down to his sheaf of corn.**
4. All of the answers are correct.

4 Why did Jacob send Joseph to Shechem? (37:14)
1. **To check on his brothers and the flocks**
2. To buy grain
3. To find the Ishmaelites
4. To sell some land

5 What did Joseph's brothers plan to do to him? (37:20)
1. To kill him
2. To throw him into a cistern
3. To say a ferocious animal devoured him
4. **All of the answers are correct.**

6 Who suggested that the brothers sell Jacob to the Ishmaelite merchants? (37:26-27)
1. Reuben
2. **Judah**
3. Asher
4. Zebulon

7 What did Joseph's brothers do to him? (37:28)
1. They killed him.
2. They left him in the cistern.
3. **They sold him to the Ishmaelites for 20 shekels of silver.**
4. They brought him home with them.

8 What did Reuben say when he discovered that Joseph was sold to the Ishmaelites? (37:30)
1. **"Where can I turn now?"**
2. "Did you kill Joseph?"
3. "How much money did you make from the sale?"
4. "Don't shed any blood."

9 How did Jacob react to the news about Joseph? (37:33-35)
1. He believed Joseph was torn to pieces by an animal.
2. His family could not comfort him.
3. He said he would go to the grave mourning.
4. **All of the answers are correct.**

10 Finish this verse: "The LORD is close to the brokenhearted..." (Psalm 34:18)
1. "...and comforts those in pain."
2. "...and blesses those who believe in him."
3. **"...and saves those who are crushed in spirit."**
4. "...and brings peace to those who need it."

STUDY 15

Genesis 40:1-23
Faithful and Not Forgotten

Memory Verse
"For the LORD gives wisdom; from his mouth come knowledge and understanding."
(Proverbs 2:6)

Biblical Truth
God does not abandon us in the midst of difficult times in our lives.

Teaching Tip
As you lead the Bible study, take time to explain the interpretation of Joseph's dreams. Help children to understand why these dreams made his brothers angry.

BIBLICAL COMMENTARY

In Egypt, Joseph became a slave in the house of Potiphar. While Joseph was there, Potiphar wrongfully sent him to the prison. This lesson finds Joseph as a slave in the prison. Pharaoh sent some of his workers to prison, and Joseph's new assignment was to help them.

God did not reveal his purpose to Joseph. Despite Joseph's problems, he continued to show a high level of character and of leadership. God allowed Joseph to develop his character and his devotion to God while Joseph was a slave in the prison.

Even though the cupbearer forgot Joseph, God did not. Soon, Joseph will need every lesson that he learned in his life.

WORDS OF OUR FAITH

to be **faithful** -- to be loyal, dependable, and trustworthy

ACTIVITY

You will need these items for this activity:
- 2 pitchers of water
- 2 cups
- 2 empty larger pitchers or larger buckets
- towels

Before class, place the pitchers of water at one end

of the room. Place the empty pitchers or empty buckets at the opposite end. Place some towels by the empty pitchers.

Form two teams, and instruct them to form a line behind the pitchers of the water. Give the first person on each team a cup.

Say, **Today you will have the opportunity to be a cupbearer. Fill the cup with water from the pitcher. Take the cup to the other end of the room, and pour the water into your team's pitcher or bucket. If you spill any water, you must wait for a teammate to wipe up the water before you continue. Then hurry back to the line, and give the cup to the next person to fill. Continue the relay until your team's pitcher is empty, and all of the water is in your pitcher or bucket.**

After the game, say, **There is a cupbearer in our Bible study today. We will learn what happened to him.**

BIBLICAL LESSON

Prepare a Bible story based on the lesson's scripture verses. Children will understand the lesson better if you tell them the story rather than reading it to them. A simpler version of this story is printed in the back of this book, on pages 132-133. This story is easier to read and understand.

After the story, encourage the children to discuss the story by asking the following questions. This will help them apply it to their lives. There may not be a right or wrong answer.

1. **Have you ever had a dream that you did not understand?** Encourage the children to think about the dreams they experienced. Ask, **Is there one dream that you always remember? What do you think it meant? How did it affect you?**
2. **Have you ever done something nice for someone who forgot to repay the favour?**
3. **How does the memory verse, Proverbs 2:6, relate to this story?**

Say, **We had two exciting stories today! One story is about a cupbearer, and the other story is about a baker. Both men worked for the pharaoh of Egypt.**

Joseph lived a difficult life. He endured difficult situations in Egypt, but he stayed faithful to God. God worked through Joseph to interpret these two dreams.

God did not abandon Joseph. God will not abandon us when we face difficult times in our lives.

MEMORY VERSE

Practice the study's memory verse. You will find suggestions for memory verse activities on pages 110-111.

ADDITIONAL ACTIVITIES

Choose from these options to enhance the children's Bible study.

1. Divide the children into two teams. Provide a space for children to

draw. On small pieces of paper, write some words from the story, such as cup, vine, branches, grape, bread, bird, basket, and tree. Let one member from each team select a paper and draw the object for his or her team. Allow one minute for the team to guess the object.

2. Create a skit to tell the story of Joseph, the cupbearer, the baker, and Pharaoh. Children may perform the skit for their families or for another class.

QUESTIONS FOR BASIC COMPETITION

To prepare the children for competition, read Genesis 40:1-23 to them.

1 Whom did Pharaoh put in the prison? (40:2-3)
1. The chief cupbearer
2. The chief baker
3. **Both answers are correct.**

2 Why were the faces of the cupbearer and the baker sad? (40:7-8)
1. No one took care of them in the prison.
2. **They had dreams, and no one could interpret them.**
3. They were afraid of the guards.

3 What did the men tell to Joseph? (40:8, 16)
1. **Their dreams**
2. Their innocence
3. Pharaoh's cruelty

4 Who dreamed about the vine and the grapes? (40:9-10)
1. Joseph
2. The captain of the guard
3. **The chief cupbearer**

5 What would happen to the chief cupbearer? (40:13)
1. **Pharaoh would restore him to his position.**
2. Pharaoh would kill him.
3. He would stay in the prison for two more years.

6 Who dreamed about the baskets of bread? (40:16)
1. The chief cupbearer
2. **The chief baker**
3. Pharaoh

7 What would happen to the chief baker? (40:19)
1. He would become the captain of the guard.
2. **Pharaoh would kill him.**
3. Pharaoh would restore him to his position.

8 What happened three days after Joseph interpreted the dreams? (40:20)
1. It was Pharaoh's birthday.
2. Pharaoh gave a feast for all of his officials.
3. **Both answers are correct.**

9 Whom did Pharaoh restore? (40:21)
1. **The chief cupbearer**
2. The chief baker
3. Joseph

10 What did the cupbearer forget? (40:23)
1. He forgot to tell his wife and children about his dream.
2. **He forgot to tell Pharaoh about Joseph.**
3. He forgot to bow before the Pharaoh.

QUESTIONS FOR ADVANCED COMPETITION

To prepare children for competition, read Genesis 40:1-23 to them.

1 In the prison, to whom were the cupbearer and the baker assigned? (40:4)

1. The captain of the guard
2. Pharaoh
3. **Joseph**
4. All of the answers are correct.

2 Why did the cupbearer and the baker have sad faces in the prison? (40:7-8)

1. Joseph doubled the amount of their work.
2. **They had dreams for which they did not have an interpretation.**
3. The captain of the guard gave bad news to them.
4. All of the answers are correct.

3 To whom did Joseph say interpretations belong? (40:8)

1. Pharaoh
2. Joseph
3. **God**
4. Magicians

4 What happened after the cupbearer saw a vine with three branches? (40:9-11)

1. The branches died, but the grapes still grew.
2. Grapes grew only on one branch.
3. Each branch had grapes, but there was no cup for the grapes.
4. **The buds blossomed into grapes, and he squeezed the grapes into Pharaoh's cup.**

5 What did Joseph ask the cupbearer to do for him? (40:14)

1. To remember him
2. To show him kindness
3. To mention him to Pharaoh
4. **All of the answers are correct.**

6 What did Joseph do to deserve his life in a dungeon? (40:15)

1. He killed someone.
2. **Nothing. He was innocent.**
3. He did something very bad.
4. He disobeyed a law.

7 What did the baker's dream mean? (40:18-19)

1. **In three days, Pharaoh would kill the baker.**
2. Each basket represented one year in prison.
3. The baker would never leave the prison.
4. In three days, Pharaoh would forgive the baker.

8 What happened on the third day? (40:20-22)

1. Pharaoh gave a feast for his birthday.
2. Pharaoh restored the chief cupbearer.
3. Pharaoh killed the baker.
4. **All of the answers are correct.**

9 What happened to Joseph? (40:23)

1. The chief baker forgot him.
2. **The chief cupbearer forgot him.**
3. He died in the prison.
4. His brothers came to rescue him.

10 Finish this verse: "For the LORD gives wisdom; from his mouth come..." (Proverbs 2:6)

1. **"...knowledge and understanding."**
2. "...kind words."
3. "...words of support."
4. "...understanding and blessing."

STUDY 16

Promoted!

Memory Verse

"'I cannot do it,' Joseph replied to Pharaoh, 'but God will give Pharaoh the answer he desires.'" (Genesis 41:16)

Biblical Truth

God honours those who are faithful to him.

Teaching Tip

Help children to understand that the Pharaoh, like many leaders, was sheltered from people who sought to communicate with him. Pharaoh employed advisors and only listened to them. They filtered the messages, and Pharaoh would only receive the most important news. But, God found a way to communicate to Pharaoh exactly what he needed to know, through a dream. Those who protected the leader of Egypt could not censor a dream.

BIBLICAL COMMENTARY

In Study 8, God told Abraham that another nation would enslave his descendants for 400 years. However, God would rescue them. In this chapter, that begins to happen. Joseph was a major part of God's plan.

In this study, Joseph confronted a difficult challenge. He had the choice to take credit for the interpretation of the dreams, or to acknowledge that God was the one who provided the meaning of the dreams. Joseph decided to give credit to God. Joseph knew that Pharaoh controlled Joseph's life and his freedom. However, Joseph also trusted that God would be with him regardless of what happened.

In one sense, this is a story about how Joseph gains power and fame. But Joseph's story is part of a larger one about how God fulfilled the covenant with Abraham. Joseph was a direct descendant of Abraham, and he was a slave in Egypt. A famine approached. God needed a faithful man in a vital position. Joseph became the second person in command of Egypt. Only Pharaoh was higher in status.

This study will look at the early part of Joseph's story. Later, the students will learn about how God led Joseph's family to Egypt so that they could survive the upcoming famine.

WORDS OF OUR FAITH

to show **honour** -- to show respect to someone. We honour God when we say good things about him. We also honour God when we love and obey him.

ACTIVITY

You will need this item for this activity:

- masking tape, or another way to create a boundary

Before class, use tape to mark a large square in the centre of the room. The square should be large enough to accommodate all of the children. Another option is to take the children outside to play this game.

Say, **Pharaoh, the leader of Egypt, had two dreams. One of Pharaoh's dreams had cows in it. In this game, some players will pretend to be cows. The other players will try to catch the cows.**

Choose three children to catch the cows. These children must stay in the centre area. The other children stand on one side of the room or outside the centre area.

When you give the signal to start, the other children must cross the centre section. The three children in the centre will try to tag them. When a cow-catcher tags a cow, the child must remain inside the square. These cows are not allowed to help or hinder the cow-catchers.

The game is over when all of the cows are in the centre or the time for this activity is finished.

BIBLICAL LESSON

Prepare a Bible story based on the lesson's scripture verses. Children will understand the lesson better if you tell them the story rather than reading it to them. A simpler version of this story is printed in the back of this book, on pages 133-135. This story is easier to read and understand.

After the story, encourage the children to discuss the story by asking the following questions. This will help them apply it to their lives. There may not be a right or wrong answer.

1. **God gave Pharaoh a message. Have you ever received a message from God? How did you react?**
2. **Joseph was in prison for two years before he heard about Pharaoh's dream. Have you ever waited a long time for God or someone else to fulfil a promise? How did you feel?**
3. **Joseph said that he could not interpret dreams. Instead, he said that God could do this. How do you give God credit for the things he does in your life?**

Say, **God honoured Joseph's faithfulness when he revealed to him the meaning of Pharaoh's dreams. Even though life was difficult for Joseph, God remembered him. Suddenly, Joseph's situation improved dramatically.**

Have you ever experienced such a quick improvement in your life? God blessed Joseph because of his faithfulness. God honours us for our faithfulness to Him.

MEMORY VERSE

Practice the study's memory verse. You will find suggestions for memory verse activities on pages 110-111.

ADDITIONAL ACTIVITIES

Choose from these options to enhance the children's Bible study.

1. As a class, find three Bible verses that talk about God's care for his people.
2. Find a map of Egypt. As a class, research some facts about the nation of Egypt today.
3. Create a news story that tells about the appointment of Joseph as the second-in-command to Pharaoh. Write this story for presentation on television, radio, or the internet.

QUESTIONS FOR BASIC COMPETITION

To prepare the children for competition, read Genesis 41:1-57 to them.

1 About what did Pharaoh dream? (41:2-7)
1. The cupbearer and Joseph
2. The cows and the corn
3. Both answers are correct.

2 What did the ugly cows do in Pharaoh's dream? (41:4)
1. They stayed in the river.
2. They ate the good corn.
3. They ate the fat cows.

3 What happened to the seven healthy heads of corn? (41:7)
1. The seven thin heads of corn swallowed them.
2. The cows swallowed them.
3. They became scorched.

4 Whom did Pharaoh ask first to interpret his dreams? (41:8)
1. The chief cupbearer
2. The magicians and the wise men
3. Both answers are correct.

5 Why did Pharaoh send for Joseph? (41:9-15)
1. The cupbearer told Pharaoh about Joseph.
2. Pharaoh heard that Joseph interpreted some dreams.
3. Both answers are correct.

6 Who did Joseph say would give Pharaoh the answer he desired? (41:16)
1. God
2. Joseph
3. The magicians

7 What would God do in Egypt? (41:29-32)
1. He would bring seven years of the abundance.
2. He would bring seven years of the famine after the years of the abundance.
3. Both answers are correct.

8 What did Joseph say that Pharaoh should do? (41:33-35)
1. To begin to buy the grain from other countries
2. To collect the grain during the abundant years
3. To save the water in the wells

9 Why did Pharaoh put Joseph in charge of the grain? (41:39-40)
1. God told Joseph everything about the famine.
2. There was no one as discerning and wise as Joseph.
3. Both answers are correct.

10 Why did all of the countries come to Egypt to buy grain from Joseph? (41:57)
1. The famine was severe in all of the world.
2. The grain in Egypt was the best in the world.
3. Both answers are correct.

QUESTIONS FOR ADVANCED COMPETITION

To prepare children for competition, read Genesis 41:1-57 to them.

1 Why was Pharaoh troubled? (41:2-8)
1. Egypt declared a war on an enemy.
2. **Pharaoh had two dreams that his magicians could not interpret.**
3. Pharaoh could not sleep.
4. Pharaoh heard a bad report about an official.

2 For whom did Pharaoh send to interpret his dreams? (41:8)
1. **The magicians and wise men**
2. The priests
3. The doctors
4. The cupbearer

3 Why did Pharaoh ask for Joseph? (41:9-14)
1. The captain of the guard told Pharaoh about Joseph.
2. The magician asked for Joseph.
3. **The cupbearer remembered Joseph.**
4. God told Pharaoh about Joseph.

4 What did Pharaoh say to Joseph when Joseph came before him? (41:14-15)
1. "Help the wise men with my dream."
2. "You are a prisoner! You can not help me."
3. "If you are wrong, you will return to the prison."
4. **"When you hear a dream, you can interpret it."**

5 What did Joseph say to Pharaoh after he heard his dreams? (41:25, 32)
1. "God revealed to Pharaoh what he will do."
2. "It is one and the same dream."
3. "God will do it soon."
4. **All of the answers are correct.**

6 What happened to Joseph? (41:41, 45, 50)
1. Pharaoh put him in charge of Egypt.
2. He received a wife.
3. He had two sons.
4. **All of the answers are correct.**

7 Who was Joseph's wife? (41:45)
1. Rebekah
2. Zilpah
3. **Asenath**
4. Bilhah

8 What happened after seven years of the abundance? (41:53-54)
1. The famine happened only in Egypt.
2. **The famine began as Joseph said.**
3. The famine lasted seven months.
4. All of the answers are correct.

9 What did Pharaoh say to those who wanted food? (41:55)
1. "We have no more food."
2. "I will not give you food."
3. "Take this and eat it."
4. **"Go to Joseph, and do what he tells you."**

10 Finish this verse: "'I cannot do it,' Joseph replied to Pharaoh, 'but God...'" (Genesis 41:16)
1. "'...will give you more dreams.'"
2. **"'...will give Pharaoh the answer he desires.'"**
3. "'...will tell me what to say.'"
4. "'...can do all things.'"

STUDY 17

Are you Spies?

Memory Verse

"I am with you and will watch over you wherever you go, and I will bring you back to this land. I will not leave you until I have done what I have promised you." (Genesis 28:15)

Biblical Truth

We honour God when we obey him.

Teaching Tip

Point out that Joseph used an interpreter when he met with his brothers. Help the children realize that they did not recognize Joseph, and they did not know he could understand what they were saying. Joseph had a great advantage as he decided how to deal with them.

BIBLICAL COMMENTARY

The covenant God established with Abraham in Genesis 15 was threatened many times throughout history. In this story, the famine had the potential to kill Jacob and his family and halt the lineage of Abraham. However, God fulfilled his promise. Jacob's heirs remained alive. Also, Jacob's family went to Egypt to buy food along with other Canaanites.

Joseph controlled the lives of his brothers. They bowed before Joseph as his dreams predicted. Joseph had a choice to make. Would he get revenge on his brothers, or would he show grace to them in their time of need?

Verse 24 gives a glimpse into Joseph's thoughts. Joseph wept as his brothers recalled their sin against him. Yet, Joseph was unsure of their motives. Joseph had a plan to test the strength and honesty of these men. How would they respond? Did they learn their lesson?

Study 18 will continue to reveal God's plan and Joseph's obedience in one of the most memorable family dramas in the Bible.

ACTIVITY

The teacher will play the role of Joseph. Stand and face the students. Say, **I am Joseph. I will give to you instructions to do various actions, and I want you to imitate my actions. Listen for these words: "Joseph says." Imitate** only the actions that follow the words "Joseph says." If I say, "Joseph says, 'Raise your hand,'" then imitate my action. If I say, "Raise you hand," do not imitate my action because I did not say, "Joseph says."

Practice a few times to make sure that the children understand how to play the game. Use various commands and demonstrate the actions. Sometimes, begin with "Joseph says."

These commands can include the following actions: pat your head, smile, wave hello, flex your muscles, touch your toes, turn around, and sit down. You may add your own commands to make the game longer.

Say, **In this activity you listened to the command. Then you decided whether to imitate my action. When I said, "Joseph says," you imitated my action because I was in charge. I had power.**

Today we will learn that Joseph had power over Egypt. We will learn what he did with that power.

BIBLICAL LESSON

Prepare a Bible story based on the lesson's scripture verses. Children will understand the lesson better if you tell them the story rather than reading it to them. A simpler version of this story is printed in the back of this book, on pages 136-138. This story is easier to read and understand.

After the story, encourage the children to discuss the story by asking the following questions. This will help them apply it to their lives. There may not be a right or wrong answer.

1. **Has anyone wronged you and later needed your help? What did you do?**
2. **When the brothers found the silver in the sack, they asked, "What is this that God has done to us?" Did God really do that to them? Have you ever blamed God for your troubles?**
3. **Why do you think Joseph's brothers did not recognize him?**

Say, **Joseph experienced a difficult life. His brothers hated him, and they sold him to merchants who took him to a foreign land. He worked as a household slave, and he unjustly became a prisoner. Through all of this, God was with Joseph. God worked to save Joseph's family and to bring healing and peace to Joseph's brothers.**

Joseph was now in a place of authority. How would Joseph respond when his brothers learned who he was?

Everyone makes choices. We can bring honour to God by making right choices. Joseph brought honour to God by his choices and his attitude.

MEMORY VERSE

Practice the study's memory verse. You will find suggestions on page 110-111.

ADDITIONAL ACTIVITIES

Choose from these options to enhance the children's Bible study.

1. As a group, find answers to these questions: What is a famine? What causes a famine? What effect does a famine have on the economy and on the people? Is there a famine anywhere in the world now? How can you help people who experience famine? Help children prepare a report on their research.

2. Ask, **Why did Joseph's brothers not recognize him? How did Joseph recognize his brothers? How did their actions fulfil Joseph's dreams?** Have children act out this story with dialogue that answers these questions.

QUESTIONS FOR BASIC COMPETITION

To prepare the children for competition, read Genesis 42:1-38 to them.

1 Which brother did not go to Egypt? (42:4)
1. Simeon
2. **Benjamin**
3. Reuben

2 Why did Jacob not want to send Benjamin to Egypt? (42:4)
1. **Harm might come to Benjamin.**
2. Benjamin was sick.
3. Benjamin watched the flocks.

3 In front of whom did the brothers bow down? (42:6)
1. The governor
2. Joseph
3. **Both answers are correct.**

4 Who was recognized when the brothers asked Joseph for food? (42:8)
1. Joseph and his brothers recognized each other.
2. **Joseph recognized his brothers, but they did not recognize him.**
3. Joseph did not recognize his brothers.

5 What did Joseph say his brothers were? (42:14)
1. **Spies**
2. Shepherds
3. His brothers

6 Why did Joseph keep one of his brothers in the prison while the other brothers returned to their home? (42:16-20)
1. They told Joseph that they were spies.
2. **Joseph wanted to learn if they told the truth.**
3. They did not pay for their grain.

7 When did Joseph weep? (42:21-24)
1. **His brothers said they received punishment for what they did to Joseph.**
2. He received bad news from Pharaoh.
3. Both answers are correct.

8 What did the brothers find in their sacks of grain? (42:27)
1. **Their silver**
2. Stolen jewels from the home of Joseph
3. Both answers are correct.

9 What did Jacob say when Joseph's brothers told him what happened? (42:36)
1. **"Everything is against me."**
2. "If I must send Benjamin, I will."
3. "Why did the governor put you in prison?"

10 Who promised to bring back Benjamin? (42:37)
1. Simeon
2. **Reuben**
3. Jacob

QUESTIONS FOR ADVANCED COMPETITION

To prepare children for competition, read Genesis 42:1-38 to them.

1 What happened because of the famine in Canaan? (42:3-5)
1. People from Canaan went to Egypt to buy grain.
2. Jacob sent 10 of his sons to Egypt.
3. Jacob did not send Benjamin with his brothers.
4. **All of the answers are correct.**

2 What happened when the brothers arrived in Egypt? (42:7-9)
1. Joseph would not sell grain to them.
2. **Joseph said that they were spies.**
3. Joseph would not see them.
4. There was no more grain.

3 What did Joseph do after his brothers said they were honest men? (42:11-17)
1. He asked them trick questions to test their statements.
2. He sent them to their home right away.
3. **He put them in the prison for three days.**
4. He made them prove that they were shepherds.

4 What happened to Joseph's brothers after three days in the prison? (42:24)
1. All of the 10 brothers went back to Canaan.
2. Reuben became a slave in Joseph's household.
3. Jacob came to Egypt to get them out of the prison.
4. **Nine brothers went to their home, but one brother stayed in Egypt.**

5 Which brother did Joseph have bound and taken from them before their eyes? (42:24)
1. Rueben
2. Benjamin
3. **Simeon**
4. Levi

6 What orders did Joseph give when it was time for the brothers to leave? (42:25)
1. To fill their bags with some grain
2. To put back the silver in the sack of each man
3. To give to them some provisions for their journey
4. **All of the answers are correct.**

7 When the brothers returned to the land of Canaan, what did they tell Jacob? (42:29)
1. Nothing
2. Simeon was dead.
3. **Everything that happened to them**
4. They lost their way on the journey.

8 What did Rueben try to convince Jacob to do? (42:36-37)
1. **To allow Benjamin to come with them to Egypt**
2. To send more money to buy some grain
3. To come to Egypt also
4. All of the answers are correct.

9 What did Jacob do after Reuben tried to convince him to let Benjamin go to Egypt? (42:38)
1. He said that Benjamin was the only son of Rachel who was alive.
2. He said that if someone harmed Benjamin, he would die in sorrow.
3. He would not permit Benjamin to go.
4. **All of the answers are correct.**

10 Finish this verse: "I am with you and will watch over you wherever you go, and I will bring you back to this land. I will not leave you until I have done..." (Genesis 28:15).
1. **"...what I have promised you."**
2. "...miraculous things."
3. "...all that you need."
4. "...all these things and more."

STUDY 18

Face to Face

Memory Verse
"Be kind and compassionate to one another, forgiving each other, just as in Christ God forgave you." (Ephesians 4:32)

Biblical Truth
God forgives us, and he wants us to forgive others.

Teaching Tip
• Help children understand why Joseph and Benjamin were different from the other sons. Tell the children that Joseph and Benjamin were Jacob's favourite sons because they were sons of Rachel, his favourite wife. In this story, it is clear that Jacob is still heartbroken over the loss of Joseph. He does not want to risk losing Benjamin as well.
• Remind children that Israel was the name that God gave to Jacob after they struggled.

BIBLICAL COMMENTARY

Israel instructed his sons to return to Egypt and to buy more food. This seemed simple, but Judah reminded his father that Joseph commanded them to return with Benjamin.

Israel was old and desperate. He spoke of trouble, bereavement, mistakes, and mercy. When Israel had no other choices left, he agreed to send his sons back to Egypt. He said that he would die of sorrow if Benjamin did not return safely. As the brothers watched their father's lament, they felt guilty. The brothers were responsible for the loss of Joseph. Could they guarantee the safe return of Benjamin?

In Egypt, Joseph was kind toward his family, but he was resolute in his plan. Joseph did not plan revenge on his brothers, but he tested their attitudes. Joseph wondered if his brothers treated Benjamin as they treated him. Were the brothers truly repentant?

Judah promised his life for Benjamin's safety. Judah asked that Joseph take him as a slave instead of Benjamin. In the crisis, the brothers revealed their attitudes.

WORDS OF OUR FAITH

mercy -- forgiveness or kindness to those who did what was wrong.

compassion -- concern for others that leads us to help them.

the **steward** -- a trusted member of Joseph's household. He was in charge of Joseph's house and business affairs.

bereavement -- a sad feeling because someone very close has died.

divination -- a way to discover knowledge through the study of objects, signs, or supernatural powers.

ACTIVITY

You will need these items for this activity:

- a cup
- a piece of wood
- two boxes

Before class, place the piece of wood in one box. Place the cup in the other box. Close the boxes. You can cover them with a cloth or close the top of the box. Make sure that a child cannot see what is inside the boxes.

Divide the class into teams. Say, **Today we will try to find a cup. One of these boxes has a cup inside. The other box has a piece of wood. Each team will take a turn as it sends a member to choose one of the boxes. If a player chooses the box with the block of wood, the player returns to the team. If the player chooses the box with the cup, the player must go to the other team and become a member of that team.**

Let each child take a turn, as time permits. After every turn, replace the items in each box. Do not let the children see.

At the end of the game, count the team members. The team with the most members is the winner.

Say, **The brothers of Joseph found a silver cup in Benjamin's bag. Joseph said that the person who owned that bag would become his slave.**

BIBLICAL LESSON

Prepare a Bible story based on the lesson's scripture verses. Children will understand the lesson better if you tell them the story rather than reading it to them. A simpler version of this story is printed in the back of this book, on pages 138-139. This story is easier to read and understand.

After the story, encourage the children to discuss the story by asking the following questions. This will help them apply it to their lives. There may not be a right or wrong answer.

1. **Judah promised to protect Benjamin. Have you ever had a friend, a brother, or a sister whom you protected? How did you feel about that person?**
2. **Joseph did not reveal his identity to his brothers. Why not? How do you treat people who have done wrong things to you?**
3. **Joseph was emotionally moved by the sight of his brother, Benjamin. Have you ever seen something that made you cry? Did you ever cry when you saw someone? Talk about this experience.**

4. Have you ever watched someone suffer? Did that person hurt you in the past? Were you tempted to hurt the person, even though he or she needed help?

Say, **Joseph had this choice. His brothers sold him into slavery, and they lied to his father. Now they were at his mercy. He recognized them, but they did not recognize him.**

Joseph had the authority to condemn his brothers to death. However, he chose not to take revenge on them.

God forgives us, and he wants us to forgive others. God will help us forgive others and resolve our conflicts.

MEMORY VERSE

Practice the study's memory verse. You will find suggestions on page 110-111.

ADDITIONAL ACTIVITIES

Choose from these options to enhance the children's Bible study.

1. Have the children dramatize the search through the sacks. You can use the items from the activity earlier in this lesson.
2. Judah offered to replace Benjamin as Joseph's slave. He asked to take the place of Benjamin. How is this similar to the way Jesus became a sacrifice for our sins?
3. Research the distance between Egypt and Israel. How far did Joseph's brothers need to travel? Draw their route on a map.

QUESTIONS FOR BASIC COMPETITION

To prepare the children for competition, read Genesis 43:1-15, 23b-32; 44:1-18, 33-34 to them.

1 Why did Israel send his sons back to Egypt? (43:1-2)

1. The famine was still severe.
2. They ate all of the grain that they had.
3. **Both answers are correct.**

2 Who said he would bring Benjamin back safely? (43:8-9)

1. Israel
2. **Judah**
3. Simeon

3 What did the brothers bring to give to Joseph? (43:11-13)

1. The silver that was put in their sacks
2. The gifts they brought
3. **Both answers are correct.**

4 Who took the brothers to Joseph's house? (43:24)

1. **Joseph's steward**
2. The captain of the guard
3. Joseph

5 About whom did Joseph ask the brothers? (43:26-27)

1. Simeon
2. Reuben
3. **Their father**

6 Which brother caused Joseph to be moved deeply? (43:29-30)

1. **Benjamin**
2. Simeon
3. Judah

7 What did the steward put in Benjamin's sack? (44:1-2)

1. Silver
2. Joseph's silver cup
3. **Both answers are correct.**

8 What happened after the brothers left Egypt? (44:4)

1. Traders sold them more grain.
2. **Joseph sent his steward after them.**
3. Thieves stole their grain.

9 Why did the brothers throw themselves at Joseph's feet? (44:14-16)

1. They thought all of them would die.
2. **They thought all of them would become slaves.**
3. Both answers are correct.

10 What did Judah say to Joseph? (44:33)

1. Let me become your slave instead of the boy.
2. Let the boy return with his brothers.
3. **Both answers are correct.**

QUESTIONS FOR ADVANCED COMPETITION

To prepare children for competition, read Genesis 43:1-15, 23b-32; 44:1-18, 33-34 to them.

1 Why did the brothers return to Egypt? (43:1-2)
1. They had a plan to rescue Simeon.
2. **The famine was still severe, and the family ate all of the grain.**
3. They needed to find work.
4. All of the answers are correct.

2 Which brother promised to bring back Benjamin safely? (43:8-9)
1. Simeon
2. Reuben
3. **Judah**
4. Levi

3 What did the brothers bring as a gift for Joseph? (43:11)
1. Pistachio nuts
2. Myrrh
3. Some honey
4. **All of the answers are correct.**

4 What did Israel say about their trip? (43:14)
1. He hoped that God Almighty would grant mercy to them.
2. He hoped that Simeon would come back with them.
3. He hoped that Benjamin would come back with them.
4. **All of the answers are correct.**

5 Where did the brothers go to prepare for Joseph's arrival? (43:24)
1. The palace of Pharaoh
2. The prison
3. **The house of Joseph**
4. A storage place for the grain

6 What did Joseph want to know? (43:27)
1. **Was their father still alive?**
2. Did they return the silver from their grain sacks?
3. Did his servants return Simeon safely to his brothers?
4. All of the answers are correct.

7 What moved Joseph deeply? (43:30)
1. The sight of Simeon out of the prison
2. The gifts and the silver that the brothers presented to him
3. The bowing of his brothers before him
4. **The sight of his own brother, Benjamin**

8 What did the brothers say when Joseph's steward stopped them? (44:7)
1. "Why did you follow us?"
2. **"Far be it from your servants to do anything like that!"**
3. "We did not take anything."
4. "Where is your master?"

9 Why did the brothers throw themselves at Joseph's feet? (44:14-16)
1. They were afraid that they would be slaves.
2. They were innocent of the theft of Joseph's cup.
3. They did not want Benjamin to become a slave.
4. **All of the answers are correct.**

10 Finish this verse: "Be kind and compassionate to one another, forgiving each other..." (Ephesians 4:32)
1. "...with patience and love."
2. "...whenever someone asks."
3. **"...just as in Christ God forgave you."**
4. "...and living in Christ."

STUDY 19

Memory Verse

"But God sent me ahead of you to preserve for you a remnant on earth and to save your lives by a great deliverance." (Genesis 45:7)

Biblical Truth

God works through the people who obey him.

Teaching Tip

Remind children how Joseph's brothers treated him in the past. Help them understand why the brothers would be terrified at his presence (see 45:3).

BIBLICAL COMMENTARY

Joseph knew that his brothers had changed their attitudes! Emotions overcame him as he made his revelation to his brothers, "I am Joseph!" Joseph acknowledged the sin of his brothers, but he did not condemn them or punish them. Joseph acknowledged that God worked through the entire series of events. He said, "Do not be angry with yourselves for selling me here, because it was to save lives that God sent me ahead of you." He truly forgave his brothers, and he affirmed God's care for him.

Pharaoh told Joseph to bring his entire family to Egypt, where Pharaoh would give them the best of the land. The brothers returned to their father with the good news that Joseph was alive. There was anticipation of a grand and glorious reunion between Joseph and his father. Jacob eagerly planned to leave Canaan and to go to Egypt.

WORDS OF OUR FAITH

a **remnant** -- a small group that survives an event that destroyed the majority of the people.

ACTIVITY

You will need this item for this activity:
- a blindfold

Say, **Sometimes we recognize people by their voices.**

Can you tell who someone is when you hear his or her voice? Our game today will give you the opportunity to do that.

Place a blindfold on one child. Choose another child to call out, "Here I am. Who am I?" The caller may try to disguise his or her voice. The blindfolded child must guess the name of the caller. If the blindfolded child does not guess the first time, have the caller give a hint. As time permits, allow every child who wants to play to have a turn.

Ask, **What made it difficult to recognize a voice?** (The voice was not clear, it sounded different, or the blindfolded child could not remember the caller's name.) **When we do not see people for a long time, they change so much that we do not recognize them. Sometimes we do not recognize people when we see them in an unexpected place. Have you ever experienced these things?** (Let the children respond.)

When Joseph's brothers arrived in Egypt, did they recognize him? Did they expect to find him there? Our lesson today continues the story of Joseph and his brothers.

BIBLICAL LESSON

Prepare a Bible story based on the lesson's scripture verses. Children will understand the lesson better if you tell them the story rather than reading it to them. A simpler version of this story is printed in the back of this book, on pages 139-141. This story is easier to read and understand.

After the story, encourage the children to discuss the story by asking the following questions. This will help them apply it to their lives. There may not be a right or wrong answer.

1. **What is the biggest surprise that you experienced?**
2. **Why do you think the brothers were scared when they realized who Joseph was? How would you feel?**
3. **Joseph had mercy on his brothers. Has anyone been merciful to you? Do you think you deserved mercy?**

Say, **God worked to bring this family together. Joseph had a godly attitude, because he loved and obeyed God. The brothers received mercy even though they deserved punishment. God worked in the lives of Joseph's family, and he still works in our lives today.**

MEMORY VERSE

Practice the study's memory verse. You will find suggestions on page 110-111.

ADDITIONAL ACTIVITIES

Choose from these options to enhance the children's Bible study.

1. Create a family tree for Joseph. Include his wife, children, brothers, parents, and grandparents.
2. Have each child create a family tree for his or her family. Have the chil-

dren research the names of their grandparents and great-grandparents as far back as they are able.

3. Make a timeline of everything that happened to Joseph. Start when his father gave him the coat of many colours and end with his father's move to Egypt.

QUESTIONS FOR BASIC COMPETITION

To prepare the children for competition, read Genesis 42:1-38 to them.

1 What did Joseph do when he could no longer control himself? (45:1-3)

    1. He gave the donkeys to his brothers.

    2. He told his brothers who he was.

    3. He returned all of the brothers' silver.

2 About whom did Joseph ask his brothers? (45:3)

    1. His father

    2. His mother

    3. The children of his brothers

3 Who did Joseph say sent him to Egypt? (45:5)

    1. His brothers

    2. Jacob

    3. God

4 Why did God send Joseph ahead of his brothers? (45:7)

    1. To preserve a remnant, a small group that survives

    2. To save lives

    3. Both answers are correct.

5 What were the brothers to tell Jacob? (45:9)

    1. Joseph is the lord of all of Egypt.

    2. Come down to me; don't delay.

    3. Both answers are correct.

6 Who told Joseph to bring his father to Egypt? (45:17-18)

    1. The priests and magicians

    2. Pharaoh

    3. His brothers

7 How did Jacob respond when the brothers told him that Joseph was alive? (27:25)

    1. He was stunned, and he did not believe them.

    2. He believed them right away.

    3. Both answers are correct.

8 What did Israel decide to do after he knew that Joseph was alive? (45:28)

    1. To order Joseph to come to him

    2. To go to Egypt and to see Joseph

    3. To stay where he was

9 What happened at Beersheba? (46:1-4)

    1. Israel offered sacrifices.

    2. God told Israel not to be afraid to go to Egypt.

    3. Both answers are correct.

10 Who promised to bring Jacob back from Egypt? (46:4)

    1. God

    2. Joseph

    3. Both answers are correct.

QUESTIONS FOR ADVANCED COMPETITION

To prepare children for competition, read Genesis 42:1-38 to them.

1 How did Joseph make himself known to his brothers? (45:1-3)
1. He said, "You will pay for what you did to me!"
2. He said, "I am Joseph, and you will be my slaves!"
3. **He told everyone to leave, and he said, "I am Joseph!"**
4. All of the answers are correct.

2 How many more years of famine would occur? (45:6, 11)
1. **Five**
2. Two
3. Ten
4. Seven

3 Who did Joseph say sent him to Egypt? (45:8)
1. His brothers
2. The Ishmaelites
3. The Midianites
4. **God**

4 About what were the brothers to tell Joseph's father? (45:13)
1. The party that they enjoyed in Egypt
2. The food that the brothers grew in Egypt
3. **All of the honour accorded to Joseph in Egypt and everything that they saw**
4. News about Joseph's new family

5 How did Joseph react to Benjamin? (45:14)
1. He shook Benjamin's hand.
2. **He threw his arms around Benjamin, and he wept.**
3. He did not realize that it was Benjamin.
4. He was happy, and he spoke to Benjamin through an interpreter.

6 How did Pharaoh react to the news that Joseph's brothers came? (45:16-20)
1. He was pleased.
2. He directed Joseph to bring his family to Egypt.
3. He offered to them the best of the land of Egypt.
4. **All of the answers are correct.**

7 How did Jacob know that his sons told the truth about Joseph? (45:27-28)
1. Joseph came with them.
2. He was never sure, but he trusted them.
3. **He heard their story, and he saw the carts that Joseph sent.**
4. He did not believe them, but he decided to see for himself.

8 What did God tell Israel at Beersheba? (46:1-4)
1. "Do not be afraid.
2. "I will make you into a great nation."
3. "I will go down to Egypt with you."
4. **All of the answers are correct.**

9 What did Jacob bring with him to Egypt? (46:7)
1. His best servants
2. **All of his offspring**
3. His wife and his children
4. Only himself

10 Finish this verse: "But God sent me ahead of you to preserve for you a remnant on earth and to save your lives by a..." (Genesis 45:7)
1. **"...great deliverance."**
2. "...sacrifice."
3. "...miracle."
4. "...helpful hand."

STUDY 20

Promises Fulfilled

Memory Verse

"But God will surely come to your aid and take you up out of this land to the land he promised on oath to Abraham, Isaac and Jacob." (Genesis 50:24b)

Biblical Truth

God loves people, and keeps his promises.

Teaching Tip

Forgiveness and reconciliation are important concepts to learn. However, children also should know that God values justice and right relationships. God calls us to protect and to care for children who are harmed or abused.

BIBLICAL COMMENTARY

This study brings both resolution and unanswered questions for the family of Israel. The family was safe in Egypt from famine. However, Joseph reminded them that they would not remain in Egypt forever. The family must return to Canaan to fulfil God's promise in Genesis 15. Canaan was the land that God promised Abraham, Isaac, and Jacob.

Joseph and Jacob were reunited. However, the brothers were afraid of Joseph. Approximately 17 years passed between Jacob's arrival in Egypt and his death. During this time, the brothers lived comfortably under the protection of Joseph. However, they worried that he protected them only because Jacob was alive. Joseph forgave the brothers a long time before Jacob died. Because of this, he wept when his brothers spoke about their fear.

Did the brothers ever rid themselves of the guilt they carried? The Bible does not say. However, the lives of Joseph, Jacob, and the brothers showed the effects of true forgiveness and reconciliation. Jacob's sons demonstrated how a lack of forgiveness can bring spiritual bondage. At the end of this study, both Jacob and Joseph died.

WORDS OF OUR FAITH

to **glorify** -- to give honour or praise to someone or something.

ACTIVTY

You will need these items for this activity:

- a piece of yarn or tape

Before class, use tape or yarn to mark a path to another place in your building or area. For best results, mark a path that has several turns. Meet with your class at the beginning of the path.

Say, **Jacob needed directions to Goshen. He sent Judah to ask Joseph for directions. Today you will give me directions to a location in our area. On the ground, there is a path that is visible. You will give me directions that follow the path. Be specific!**

As the children give you directions, interpret the directions as literally as possible. Only stop when the children tell you to stop. Do not turn unless you are instructed to turn. If you are instructed to turn, rotate slowly until the children tell you to stop. Continue to follow the directions until you arrive at the destination.

Say, **Jacob followed the directions that Joseph gave to Judah. At the end of his travels, Jacob met Joseph.**

When we receive directions from God, we must follow them. God guides us to good things.

BIBLICAL LESSON

Prepare a Bible story based on the lesson's scripture verses. Children will understand the lesson better if you tell them the story rather than reading it to them. A simpler version of this story is printed in the back of this book, on pages 141-142. This story is easier to read and understand.

After the story, encourage the children to discuss the story by asking the following questions. This will help them apply it to their lives. There may not be a right or wrong answer.

1. **Joseph forgave his brothers for what they did. He did this even though the brothers did something wrong to him. Have you ever forgiven someone who did something extremely wrong against you? Was it easy or difficult? Why?**
2. **Joseph's brothers were afraid that Joseph would punish them for what they did. Have you ever felt guilty for something that you did to someone else? How did your guilt affect your relationship to that person?**

Say, **During his years in Egypt, Joseph did not know what would happen to him. However, he remained faithful to God. Joseph was very happy when he was reunited with his father.**

Like Joseph, we do not know what will happen in our lives. However, God wants us to be faithful to him. God is the main character of Genesis because he saved and healed Jacob's family. God worked through Jacob and his sons to bring the family back together again.

MEMORY VERSE

Practice the study's memory verse. You will find suggestions on page 110-111.

ADDITIONAL ACTIVITIES

Choose from these options to enhance the children's Bible study.

1. Pretend to be Joseph and his brothers. As a class, write a letter of apology from Joseph's brothers to Joseph. Then, write a letter of forgiveness from Joseph to his brothers.

2. With the information you learned, create a family tree of Abraham's family. List the descendants of Abraham, Isaac, Jacob, and Joseph.

3. Write a song about Joseph and his brothers. Use a familiar melody for the music. Write the lyrics as a class.

QUESTIONS FOR BASIC COMPETITION

To prepare the children for competition, read Genesis 46:28-32 and 50:14-26 to them.

1 How did Jacob get to Goshen? (46:28)
1. Pharaoh sent someone to show the way.
2. Joseph travelled with them.
3. **Jacob sent Judah to get the directions.**

2 When did Joseph go to Goshen? (46:29)
1. A week after Jacob arrived
2. **When Jacob arrived in Goshen**
3. Joseph never went to Goshen.

3 What happened when Joseph finally appeared before Israel? (46:29)
1. Joseph threw his arms around his father.
2. Joseph wept for a long time.
3. **Both answers are correct.**

4 After Jacob died, why did the brothers worry? (50:15)
1. **They thought that Joseph would pay them back for all the wrongs that they did to him.**
2. They thought that Pharaoh would not show kindness to them anymore.
3. Both answers are correct.

5 What did Joseph say when the brothers threw themselves before him? (50:18-19)
1. "Don't be afraid."
2. "Am I in the place of God?"
3. **Both answers are correct.**

6 What did Joseph say he would do? (50:21)
1. He would force his brothers to leave Goshen.
2. **He would provide for his brothers and for their children.**
3. He would make slaves of his brothers.

7 Who had intended everything that happened to Joseph for good? (50:20)
1. Jacob
2. **God**
3. Pharaoh

8 Where would God take Jacob's family? (50:24)
1. God told them to stay in Egypt forever.
2. **God would lead them to the land that he promised to them.**
3. Both answers are correct.

9 What did Joseph tell the sons of Israel to do when they left Egypt? (50:25)
1. To write everything that happened to them
2. **To carry his bones from Egypt to the Promised Land**
3. Both answers are correct.

10 What happened to Joseph? (50:22-23, 26)
1. He lived to see three generations of Ephraim's children.
2. He died at 110 years old.
3. **Both answers are correct.**

QUESTIONS FOR ADVANCED COMPETITION

To prepare children for competition, read Genesis 46:28-32 and 50:14-26 to them.

1 Whom did Jacob send ahead to get directions from Joseph? (46:28)
   1. **Judah**
   2. Reuben
   3. Benjamin
   4. Dan

2 What did Joseph do when Jacob arrived in the region of Goshen? (46:29)
   1. He had his chariot made ready .
   2. He went to Goshen to meet his father.
   3. He threw his arms around his father, and he wept for a long time.
   4. **All of the answers are correct.**

3 What did Joseph say to Pharaoh? (46:31-32)
   1. "My family is not welcome here."
   2. "We worship the one true God."
   3. **"The men are shepherds; they tend livestock."**
   4. "My family will not stay long."

4 What happened after Joseph and his brothers buried their father? (50:14-15)
   1. **The brothers worried that Joseph would pay back his brothers for what they did to him.**
   2. Joseph forced the brothers to leave Goshen.
   3. The brothers knew that Joseph forgave them.
   4. The brothers became officials.

5 What was Joseph's response after the brothers said they were his slaves? (50:18-21)
   1. He agreed to make them his slaves.
   2. **He told them not to be afraid; he would care for their families.**
   3. They had to prove that they were really sorry.
   4. All of the answers are correct.

6 What did Joseph say that God was going to do for his brothers? (50:24)
   1. **To come to their aid and to bring them out of Egypt**
   2. To help the brothers to become leaders in Egypt
   3. To choose Manasseh to lead the family
   4. All of the above

7 To whom did God promise the land? (50:24)
   1. Abraham
   2. Isaac
   3. Jacob
   4. **All of the answers are correct.**

8 What did Joseph make the sons of Israel swear to do? (50:25)
   1. To tell Pharaoh that they would tend his livestock
   2. To promise to tell their children all that happened
   3. **To carry his bones out of Egypt**
   4. To live always in Goshen

9 How old was Joseph when he died? (50:26)
   1. **110 years old**
   2. 115 years old
   3. 120 years old
   4. 125 years old

10 Finish this verse: "God will surely come to your aid and take you..." (Genesis 50:24b)
   1. "...to a new land he has set aside for you."
   2. **"...up out of this land to the land he promised on oath to Abraham, Isaac and Jacob."**
   3. "...to a land flowing with milk and honey."
   4. "...to your homeland."

MEMORY VERSES

The following verses are the memory verses for each lesson. You may reproduce this page and distribute it to the children for study purposes.

STUDY 1

"In the beginning God created the heavens and the earth." (Genesis 1:1).

STUDY 2

"So God created mankind in his own image, in the image of God he created them; male and female he created them." (Genesis 1:27)

STUDY 3

"[But] if you do not do what is right, sin is crouching at your door; it desires to have you, but you must rule over it." (Genesis 4:7b)

STUDY 4

"Noah was a righteous man, blameless among the people of his time, and he faithfully walked with God." (Genesis 6:9b)

STUDY 5

"As long as the earth endures, seedtime and harvest, cold and heat, summer and winter, day and night will never cease." (Genesis 8:22)

STUDY 6

"I have set my rainbow in the clouds, and it will be the sign of the covenant between me and the earth." (Genesis 9:13)

STUDY 7

"By faith Abraham, when called to go to a place he would later receive as his inheritance, obeyed and went, even though he did not know where he was going." (Hebrews 11:8)

STUDY 8

"Do not be afraid, Abram. I am your shield, your very great reward." (Genesis 15:1b)

STUDY 9

"Because you have done this and have not withheld your son, your only son, I will surely bless you." (Genesis 22:16b-17a)

STUDY 10

"I will instruct you and teach you in the way you should go; I will counsel you with my loving eye on you." (Psalm 32:8)

STUDY 11

"Even small children are known by their actions, so is their conduct really pure and right?" (Proverbs 20:11)

STUDY 12

"Whoever of you loves life and desires to see many good days, keep your tongue from evil and your lips from telling lies." (Psalm 34:12-13)

STUDY 13

"I am the God of your father Abraham. Do not be afraid, for I am with you." (Genesis 26:24b)

STUDY 14

"The LORD is close to the brokenhearted and saves those who are crushed in spirit. A righteous man may have many troubles, but the LORD delivers him from them all." (Psalm 34:18-19)

STUDY 15

"For the LORD gives wisdom; from his mouth come knowledge and understanding." (Proverbs 2:6)

STUDY 16

"'I cannot do it,' Joseph replied to Pharaoh, 'but God will give Pharaoh the answer he desires.'" (Genesis 41:16)

STUDY 17

"I am with you and will watch over you wherever you go, and I will bring you back to this land. I will not leave you until I have done what I have promised you." (Genesis 28:15)

STUDY 18

"Be kind and compassionate to one another, forgiving each other, just as in Christ God forgave you." (Ephesians 4:32)

STUDY 19

"But God sent me ahead of you to preserve for you a remnant on earth and to save your lives by a great deliverance." (Genesis 45:7)

STUDY 20

"But God will surely come to your aid and take you up out of this land to the land he promised on oath to Abraham, Isaac and Jacob." (Genesis 50:24b)

MEMORY VERSE ACTIVIES

THE REPEATER

Write one or two words of the verse on a small piece of paper. Instruct students to sit in a circle, and distribute the papers around the circle in correct verse order. Prepare more than one set of memory cards for large classes, and work in groups. The student with the first word of the verse says the first word. Then the next student says the first word and the new word. The third student says the first, second and third words, and so on. Keep repeating the verse from the beginning, adding a new word each time. After you complete the verse, have students pass their card to the person on their left and begin the game again.

BACK TO BACK

Ask two children who think that they know the memory verse to stand back to back. Ask one child to say the first word of the verse and the other child to say the next word. The children will go back and forth saying the words until someone makes a mistake. The one who missed a word sits down. The remaining child is the champi- on. Ask the whole class to say the memory verse. Then choose a new contender to compete against the champion.

WORDS AND ACTION

Using small pieces of paper, write several different activities on each one: turn around in a circle, march in place, pat your head, skip across the room, whisper, shout, say it to a friend in class. Ask each child to choose one of the cards and to do the activity listed on it while he or she recites the memory verse.

SPIDER WEB REVIEW

You will need a ball of yarn for this activity. Instruct the children to stand in a circle. Toss the ball of yarn to one child and ask him or her to say the first word of the verse. The child will wrap the yarn around his finger and toss the ball of yarn to another child across the circle. This child will say the second word of the verse and wrap the yarn around his finger. Continue playing and saying words of the verse until every child has a turn. The back and forth motion of the yarn will produce a spider web.

HIDE AND SEEK MEMORY GAME

Before the class session begins, write each word of the memory verse on a separate piece of paper. Hide the individual words around the room. Ask the children to find the words and to arrange them in the correct order. Recite the memory verse.

MISSING WORDS MEMORY GAME

You will need a chalkboard, marker board, or paper for this activity.

Write the memory verse on the chalkboard. Ask the children to recite the verse. Choose a child to erase one word, and then ask the children to repeat the verse (including the missing word.) Continue until all the words disappear, and the children say the verse from memory. If a chalkboard or marker board is not available, write each word of the verse on a separate piece of paper, and ask the children to remove one word at a time.

EASY-TO-READ VERSION OF BIBLE PASSAGES

STUDY ONE

Genesis 1:1-31; 2:2-3, 7
In the Beginning

God created the sky and the earth. At first, the earth was completely empty. There was nothing on the earth. Darkness covered the ocean, and God's Spirit moved over the water.

Then God said, "Let there be light!" And light began to shine. He saw the light, and he knew that it was good. Then he separated the light from the darkness. God named the light "day," and he named the darkness "night."

There was evening, and then there was morning. This was the first day.

Then God said, "Let there be a space to separate the water into two parts!" So God made the space and separated the water. Some of the water was above it, and some of the water was below it. God named that space "sky." There was evening, and then there was morning. This was the second day.

Then God said, "Let the water under the sky be gathered together so that the dry land will appear." And it happened. God named the dry land "earth," and he named the water that was gathered together "seas." And God saw that this was good.

Then God said, "Let the earth grow grass, plants that make grain, and fruit trees. The fruit trees will make fruit with seeds in it. And each plant will make its own kind of seed. Let these plants grow on the earth." And it happened. The earth grew grass and plants that made grain. And it grew trees that made fruit with seeds in it. Every plant made its own kind of seeds. And God saw that this was good.

There was evening, and then there was morning. This was the third day.

Then God said, "Let there be lights in the sky. These lights will separate the days from the nights. They will be used for signs to show when special meetings begin and to show the days and years. They will be in the sky to shine light on the earth." And it happened.

So God made the two large lights. He made the larger light to rule during the day and the smaller light to rule during the night. He also made the stars. God put these lights in the sky to shine on the earth. He put them in the sky to rule over the day and over the night. They separated the light from the darkness. And God saw that this was good.

There was evening, and then there was morning. This was the fourth day.

Then God said, "Let the water be filled with many living things, and let there be birds to fly in the air over the earth." So God created the large sea animals. He created all the many living things in the sea and every kind of bird that flies in the air. And God saw that this was good.

God blessed all the living things in the sea and told them to have many babies and fill the seas. And he blessed the birds on land and told them to have many more babies.

There was evening, and then there was morning. This was the fifth day.

Then God said, "Let the earth produce many kinds of living things. Let there be many different kinds of animals. Let there be large animals and small crawling animals of every kind. And let all these animals produce more animals." And all these things happened.

So God made every kind of animal. He made the wild animals, the tame animals, and all the small crawling things. And God saw that this was good.

Then God said, "Now let's make humans who will be like us. They will rule over all the fish in the sea and the birds in the air. They will rule over all the large animals and all the little things that crawl on the earth."

So God created humans in his own image. He created them to be like himself. He created them male and female. God blessed them and said to them, "Have many children. Fill the earth and take control of it. Rule over the fish in the sea and the birds in the air. Rule over every living thing that moves on the earth."

God said, "I am giving you all the grain bearing plants and all the fruit trees. These trees make fruit with seeds in it. This grain and fruit will be your food. And I am giving all the green plants to the animals. These green plants will be their food. Every animal on earth, every bird in the air, and all the little things that crawl on the earth will eat that food." And all these things happened.

God looked at everything he had made. And he saw that everything was very good.

God finished the work he was doing, so on the seventh day he rested from his work. God blessed the seventh day and made it a holy day. He made it special because on that day he rested from all the work he did while creating the world.

Then the LORD God took dust from the ground and made a man. He breathed the breath of life into the man's nose, and the man became a living thing.

STUDY TWO

Genesis 2:15-25; 3:1-24
The Problem of Sin

The LORD God put the man in the Garden of Eden to work the soil and take care of the garden. The LORD God gave him this command: "You may eat from any tree in the garden. But you must not eat from the tree that gives knowledge about good and evil. If you eat fruit from that tree, on that day you will certainly die!"

Then the LORD God said, "I see that it is not good for the man to be alone. I will make the companion he needs, one just right for him."

The LORD God used dust from the ground and made every animal in the fields and every bird in the air. He brought all these animals to the man, and the man gave them all a name. The man gave names to all the tame animals, to all the birds in the air, and to all the wild animals. He saw many animals and birds, but he could not find a companion that was right for him. So the LORD God caused the man to sleep very deeply. While he was asleep, God took one of the ribs from the man's body. Then he closed the man's skin where the rib had been. The LORD God used the rib from the man to make a woman. Then he brought the woman to the man. And the man said,

> "Finally! One like me,
>   with bones from my bones
>   and a body from my body.
>   She was taken out of a man,
>   so I will call her 'woman.'"

That is why a man leaves his father and mother and is joined to his wife. In this way two people become one.

The man and his wife were naked, but they were not ashamed.

The snake was the most clever of all the wild animals that the LORD God had made. The snake spoke to the woman and said, "Woman, did God really tell you that you must not eat from any tree in the garden?"

The woman answered the snake, "No, we can eat fruit from the trees in the garden. But there is one tree we must not eat from. God told us, 'You must not eat fruit from the tree that is in the middle of the garden. You must not even touch that tree, or you will die.'"

But the snake said to the woman, "You will not die. God knows that if you eat the fruit from that tree you will learn about good and evil, and then you will be like God!"

The woman could see that the tree was beautiful and the fruit looked so good to eat. She also liked the idea that it would make her wise. So she took some of the fruit from the tree and ate it. Her husband was there with her, so she gave him some of the fruit, and he ate it.

Then it was as if their eyes opened, and they saw things differently. They saw that they were naked. So they got some fig leaves, sewed them together, and wore them for clothes.

During the cool part of the day, the LORD God was walking in the garden. The man and the woman heard him, and they hid among the trees in the garden. The LORD God called to the man and said, "Where are you?"

The man said, "I heard you walking in the garden, and I was afraid. I was naked, so I hid."

God said to the man, "Who told you that you were naked? Did you eat fruit from that special tree? I told you not to eat from that tree!"

The man said, "The woman you put here with me gave me fruit from that tree. So I ate it."

Then the LORD God said to the woman, "What have you done?"

She said, "The snake tricked me, so I ate the fruit."

So the LORD God said to the snake,

> *"You did this very bad thing,*
> > *so bad things will happen to you.*
> *It will be worse for you*
> > *than for any other animal.*
> *You must crawl on your belly*
> > *and eat dust all the days of your life.*
> *I will make you and the woman enemies to each other.*
> > *Your children and her children will be enemies.*
> *You will bite her child's foot,*
> > *but he will crush your head."*

Then God said to the woman,

> *"I will cause you to have much trouble when you are pregnant.*
> *And when you give birth to children,*
> > *you will have much pain.*
> *You will want your husband very much,*
> > *but he will rule over you."*

Then God said to the man,

> *"I commanded you not to eat from that tree.*
> > *But you listened to your wife and ate from it.*
> *So I will curse the ground because of you.*
> > *You will have to work hard all your life for the food the ground produces. The ground will grow thorns and weeds for you.*
> > *And you will have to eat the plants that grow wild in the fields. You will work hard for your food,*
> > > *until your face is covered with sweat.*
> *You will work hard until the day you die,*
> > *and then you will become dust again.*
> *I used dust to make you,*
> > *and when you die, you will become dust again."*

Adam named his wife Eve. He gave her this name because Eve would be the mother of everyone who ever lived.

The LORD God used animal skins and made some clothes for the man and his wife. Then he put the clothes on them.

The LORD God said, "Look, the man has become like us—he knows about good and evil. And now the man might take the fruit from the tree of life. If the man eats that fruit, he will live forever."

So the LORD God forced the man out of the Garden of Eden to work the ground he was made from. God forced the man to leave the garden. Then he put Cherub angels and a sword of fire at the entrance to the garden to protect it. The sword flashed around and around, guarding the way to the tree of life.

STUDY THREE

Genesis 4:1-16, 25-26
Cain's Conflict

Adam had sexual relations with his wife Eve. She became pregnant and gave birth to a son. She named him Cain. Eve said, "With the LORD's help, I have made a man!"

Eve gave birth again to Cain's brother Abel. Abel became a shepherd, and Cain became a farmer.

At harvest time, Cain brought a gift to the LORD. He brought some of the food that he grew from the ground, but Abel brought some animals from his flock. He chose some of his best sheep and brought the best parts from them.

The LORD accepted Abel and his gift. But he did not accept Cain and his offering. Cain was sad because of this, and he became very angry. The LORD asked Cain, "Why are you angry? Why does your face look sad? You know that if you do what is right, I will accept you. But if you don't, sin is ready to attack you. That sin will want to control you, but you must control it."

Cain said to his brother Abel, "Let's go out to the field." So they went to the field. Then Cain attacked his brother Abel and killed him.

Later, the LORD said to Cain, "Where is your brother Abel?"

Cain answered, "I don't know. Is it my job to watch over my brother?"

Then the Lord said, "What have you done? You killed your brother and the ground opened up to take his blood from your hands. Now his blood is shouting to me from the ground. So you will be cursed from this ground. Now when you work the soil, the ground will not help your plants grow. You will not have a home in this land. You will wander from place to place."

Then Cain said to the LORD, "This punishment is more than I can bear! You are forcing me to leave the land, and I will not be able to be near you or have a home! Now I must wander from place to place, and anyone I meet could kill me."

Then the LORD said to Cain, "No, if anyone kills you, I will punish that person much, much more." Then the LORD put a mark on Cain to show that no one should kill him.

Cain went away from the LORD and lived in the land of Nod.

Adam again had sexual relations with his wife, and she gave birth to another son. She named him Seth. Eve said, "God has given me another son. Cain killed Abel, but now I have Seth." Seth also had a son. He named him Enosh. At that time people began to pray to the LORD.

STUDY FOUR

Genesis 6:5—7:16
One Man Obeys

The LORD saw that the people on the earth were very evil. He saw that they thought only about evil things all the time. The LORD was sorry that he had made people on the earth. It made him very sad in his heart. So the LORD said, "I will destroy all the people I created on the earth. I will destroy every person and every animal and everything that crawls on the earth. And I will destroy all the birds in the air, because I am sorry that I have made them."

But Noah pleased the LORD.

This is the history of Noah's family. He was a good man all his life, and he always followed God. Noah had three sons: Shem, Ham, and Japheth.

When God looked at the earth, he saw that people had ruined it. Violence was everywhere, and it had ruined their life on earth.

So God said to Noah, "Everyone has filled the earth with anger and violence. So I will destroy all living things. I will remove them from the earth. Use cypress wood and build a boat for yourself. Make rooms in the boat and cover it with tar inside and out.

"This is the size I want you to make the boat: 300 cubits long, 50 cubits wide, and 30 cubits high. Make a window for the boat about 1 cubit below the roof. Put a door in the side of the boat. Make three floors in the boat: a top deck, a middle deck, and a lower deck.

"Understand what I am telling you. I will bring a great flood of water on the earth. I will destroy all living things that live under heaven. Everything on the earth will die. I will make a special agreement with you. You, your wife, your sons, and their wives will all go into the boat. Also, you will take two of every living thing on the earth with you into the boat. Take a male and female of every kind of animal so that they might survive with you. Two of every kind of bird, animal, and creeping thing will come to you so that you might keep them alive. Also bring every kind of food into the boat, for you and for the animals."

Noah did everything God commanded him.

Then the LORD said to Noah, "I have seen that you are a good man, even among the evil people of this time. So gather your family, and all of you go into the boat. Get seven pairs (seven males and seven females) of every kind of clean animal. And get one pair (one male and one female) of every other animal on the earth. Lead all these animals into the boat with you. Get seven pairs (seven males and seven females) of all the birds. This will allow all these animals to continue living on the earth after the other animals are destroyed. Seven days from now, I will send much rain on the earth. It will rain for 40 days and 40 nights, and I will wipe everything off the face of the earth. I will destroy everything I made." Noah did everything the LORD told him to do.

Noah was 600 years old at the time the rains came. He and his family went into the boat to be saved from the flood. His wife and his sons and their wives were on the boat with him. All the clean animals, all the other animals on the earth, the birds, and everything that crawls on the earth went into the boat with Noah. These animals went into the boat in groups of two, male and female, just as God commanded. Seven days later the flood started. The rain began to fall on the earth.

On the 17th day of the second month, when Noah was 600 years old, the springs under the earth broke through the ground, and water flowed out everywhere. The sky also opened like windows and rain poured down. The rain fell on the earth for 40 days and 40 nights. That same day Noah went into the boat with his wife, his sons Shem, Ham, and Japheth, and their wives. They and every kind of animal on the earth were in the boat. Every kind of cattle, every kind of animal that crawls on the earth, and every kind of bird were in the boat. All these animals went into the boat with Noah. They came in groups of two from every kind of animal that had the breath of life. All these animals went into the boat in groups of two, just as God had commanded Noah. Then the LORD closed the door behind Noah.

STUDY FIVE

Genesis 7:17--8:22
The Waters Rose

Water flooded the earth for 40 days. The water began rising and lifted the boat off the ground. The water continued to rise, and the boat floated on the water high above the earth. The water rose so much that even the highest mountains were covered by the water. The water continued to rise above the mountains. The water was more than 20 feet above the highest mountain.

Every living thing on earth died—every man and woman, every bird, and every kind of animal. All the many kinds of animals and all the things that crawl on the ground died. Every living, breathing thing on dry land died. In this way God wiped the earth clean—he destroyed every living thing on the earth—every human, every animal, everything that crawls, and every bird. All that was left was Noah and his family and the animals that were with him in the boat. The water continued to cover the earth for 150 days.

But God did not forget about Noah. God remembered him and all the animals that were with him in the boat. God made a wind blow over the earth, and all the water began to disappear.

Rain stopped falling from the sky, and water stopped flowing from under the earth. The water that covered the earth began to go down. After 150 days the water was low enough that the boat touched land again. The boat stopped on one of the mountains of Ararat. This was the 17th day of the seventh month. The water continued to go down, and by the first day of the tenth month, the tops of the mountains were above the water.

Forty days later Noah opened the window he had made in the boat. Then he sent out a raven. The raven flew from place to place until the ground was dry and the water was gone. Noah also sent out a dove. He wanted it to find dry ground. He wanted to know if water still covered the earth.

The dove could not find a place to rest because water still covered the earth, so the dove came back to the boat. Noah reached out his hand and caught the dove and brought it back into the boat.

After seven days Noah again sent out the dove. And that afternoon the dove came back to Noah. The dove had a fresh olive leaf in its mouth. This was a sign to show Noah that there was dry ground on the earth. Seven days later Noah sent the dove out again. But this time the dove didn't come back.

After that Noah opened the door of the boat. He looked and saw that the ground was dry. This was the first day of the first month of the year. He was 601 years old. By the 27th day of the second month, the ground was completely dry.

Then God said to Noah, "Leave the boat. You, your wife, your sons, and your sons' wives should go out now. Bring every living animal out of the boat with you—all the birds, animals, and everything that crawls on the earth. These animals will make many more animals, and they will fill the earth again."

So Noah went out with his sons, his wife, and his sons' wives. All the animals, everything that crawls, and every bird left the boat. All the animals came out of the boat in family groups.

Then Noah built an altar to honor the LORD. Noah took some of all the clean birds and some of all the clean animals and burned them on the altar as a gift to God.

The LORD smelled these sacrifices, and it pleased him. The LORD said to himself, "I will never again curse the earth as a way to punish people. People are evil from the time they are young, but I will never again destroy every living thing on the earth as I did this time. As long as the earth continues, there will always be a time for planting and a time for harvest. There will always be cold and hot, summer and winter, day and night on earth."

STUDY SIX

Genesis 9:1-20, 28-29
The Rainbow in the Clouds

God blessed Noah and his sons and said to them, "Have many children. Fill the earth with your people. Every animal on earth, every bird in the air, every animal that crawls on the ground, and every fish in the sea will be afraid of you. All of them will be under your control. In the past, I gave you the green plants to eat. Now every animal will also be food for you. I give you everything on earth—it is yours. But I give you one command. You must not eat meat that still has its life (blood) in it. Also, I will demand your blood for your lives. That is, I will demand the life of any person or animal that takes a human life.

"God made humans to be like himself.
So whoever kills a person must be
killed by another person."

"Have many children and fill the earth with your people."

Then God said to Noah and his sons, "I

now make my promise to you and to your people who will live after you. I make my promise to all the birds, and to all the cattle, and to all the animals that came out of the boat with you. I make my promise to every living thing on earth. This is my promise to you: All life on the earth was destroyed by the flood. But that will never happen again. A flood will never again destroy all life on the earth."

And God said, "I will give you something to prove that I made this promise to you. It will continue forever to show that I have made an agreement with you and every living thing on earth. I am putting a rainbow in the clouds as proof of the agreement between me and the earth. When I bring clouds over the earth, you will see the rainbow in the clouds. When I see this rainbow, I will remember the agreement between me and you and every living thing on the earth. This agreement says that a flood will never again destroy all life on the earth. When I look and see the rainbow in the clouds, I will remember the agreement that continues forever. I will remember the agreement between me and every living thing on the earth."

So God said to Noah, "This rainbow is proof of the agreement that I made with all living things on earth."

Noah's sons came out of the boat with him. Their names were Shem, Ham, and Japheth. (Ham was the father of Canaan.) These three men were Noah's sons. And all the people on earth came from these three sons.

Noah became a farmer and planted a vineyard.

After the flood Noah lived 350 years. He lived a total of 950 years; then he died.

STUDY SEVEN

Genesis 12:1-9; 13:5-18
Calls and Choices

The LORD said to Abram, "Leave your country and your people. Leave your father's family and go to the country that I will show you.

> I will build a great nation from you.
>   I will bless you
>   and make your name famous.
> People will use your name
>   to bless other people.
> I will bless those who bless you,
>   and I will curse those who curse you.
> I will use you to bless
>   all the people on earth."

So Abram left Haran just like the LORD said, and Lot went with him. Abram was 75 years old when he left Haran. He took his wife Sarai, his nephew Lot, all the slaves, and all the other things he had gotten in Haran. Then he and his group moved to the land of Canaan. Abram traveled through the land as far as the town of Shechem and then to the big tree at Moreh. The Canaanites were living in the land at that time.

The LORD appeared to Abram and said, "I will give this land to your descendants."

Abram built an altar to honor the LORD who appeared to him there. Then he left that place and traveled to the mountains east of Bethel. He set up his tent there. Bethel was to the west, and Ai was to the east. Abram built another altar at that place to honor the LORD, and he worshiped the LORD there. Then he moved on toward the Negev, stopping for a time at several places on the way.

During this time Lot was also traveling with Abram. Lot had many animals and tents. Abram and Lot had so many animals that the land could not support both of them together. (The Canaanites and the Perizzites were also living in this land at the same time.) The shepherds of Abram and Lot began to argue.

So Abram said to Lot, "There should be no arguing between you and me or between your people and my people. We are all brothers. We should separate. You can choose any place you want. If you go to the left, I will go to the right. If you go to the right, I will go to the left."

Lot looked and saw the whole Jordan Valley. He saw that there was much water there. (This was before the LORD destroyed Sodom and Gomorrah. At that time the Jordan Valley all the way to Zoar was like the LORD's Garden. This was good land, like the land of Egypt.) So Lot chose to live in the Jordan Valley. The two men separated, and Lot began traveling east. Abram stayed in the land of Canaan, and Lot lived among the cities in the valley. Lot moved as far as Sodom and made his camp there. The LORD knew that the people of Sodom were very evil sinners.

After Lot left, the LORD said to Abram, "Look around you. Look north, south, east, west. All this land that you see I will give to you and your people who live after you. This will be your land forever. I will make your people so many that they will be like the dust of the earth. If people could count all the particles of dust on earth, they could count your people. So go. Walk through your land. I now give it to you."

So Abram moved his tents. He went to live near the big trees of Mamre. This was near the city of Hebron. There he built an altar to honor the LORD.

STUDY EIGHT

Genesis 15:1-21
Promises and Covenants

After all these things happened, the word of the LORD came to Abram in a vision. God said, "Abram, don't be afraid. I will defend you and give you a great reward."

But Abram said, "Lord GOD, there is nothing you can give me that will make me happy, because I have no son. My slave Eliezer from Damascus will get everything I own after I die." Abram said, "You have given me no son, so a slave born in my house will get everything I have."

Then the LORD spoke to Abram and said, "That slave will not be the one to get what you have. You will have a son who will get everything you own."

Then God led Abram outside and said, "Look at the sky. See the many stars. There are so many you cannot count them. Your family will be like that."

Abram believed the LORD, and because of this faith the Lord accepted him as one who has done what is right. He said to Abram, "I am the LORD who led you from Ur of Babylonia. I did this so that I could give you this land. You will own this land."

But Abram said, "Lord GOD, how can I be sure that I will get this land?"
God said to Abram, "We will make an agreement. Bring me a three-year-old cow, a three-year-old goat, a three-year-old ram, a dove, and a young pigeon."

Abram brought all these to God. Abram killed these animals and cut each of them into two pieces. Then he laid each half across from the other half. He did not cut the birds into two pieces. Later, large birds flew down to eat the animals, but Abram chased them away.

The sun began to go down and Abram got very sleepy. While he was asleep, a very terrible darkness came over him. Then the Lord said to Abram, "You should know this: Your descendants will live in a country that is not their own. They will be strangers there. The people there will make them slaves and be cruel to them for 400 years. But then I will punish the nation that made them slaves. Your people will leave that land, and they will take many good things with them.

"You yourself will live to be very old. You will die in peace and will be buried with your family. After four generations your people will come to this land again and defeat the Amorites. That will happen in the future because the Amorites are not yet guilty enough to lose their land."

After the sun went down, it got very dark. The dead animals were still on the ground, each animal cut into two pieces. Then a smoking firepot and a flaming torch passed between the halves of the dead animals.

So on that day the LORD made a promise and an agreement with Abram. He said, "I will give this land to your descendants. I will give them the land between the River of Egypt and the great river Euphrates. This is the land of the Kenites, Kenizzites, Kadmonites, Hittites, Perizzites, Rephaites, Amorites, Canaanites, Girgashites, and Jebusites."

STUDY NINE

Genesis 21:1-6; 22:1-18
Love Tested

The LORD came back to visit Sarah as he said he would, and he kept his promise to her. At exactly the time God said it would happen, Sarah became pregnant and gave birth to a son for Abraham in his old age. Abraham named his son Isaac. Abraham did what God commanded and circumcised Isaac when he was eight days old.

Abraham was 100 years old when his son Isaac was born. Sarah said, "God has made me happy, and everyone who hears about this will be happy with me.

After these things God decided to test

Abraham's faith. God said to him, "Abraham!"

And he said, "Yes!"

Then God said, "Take your son to the land of Moriah and kill your son there as a sacrifice for me. This must be Isaac, your only son, the one you love. Use him as a burnt offering on one of the mountains there. I will tell you which mountain."

In the morning Abraham got up and saddled his donkey. He took Isaac and two servants with him. He cut the wood for the sacrifice. Then they went to the place where God told them to go. After they traveled three days, Abraham looked up, and in the distance he saw the place where they were going. Then he said to his servants, "Stay here with the donkey. The boy and I will go to that place and worship. Then we will come back to you later."

Abraham took the wood for the sacrifice and put it on his son's shoulder. Abraham took the special knife and fire. Then both he and his son went together to the place for worship.

Isaac said to his father Abraham, "Father!"

Abraham answered, "Yes, son?"

Isaac said, "I see the wood and the fire. But where is the lamb we will burn as a sacrifice?"

Abraham answered, "God himself is providing the lamb for the sacrifice, my son."

So both Abraham and his son went together to that place. When they came to the place where God told them to go, Abraham built an altar. He carefully laid the wood on the altar. Then he tied up his son Isaac and laid him on the altar on top of the wood. Then Abraham reached for his knife to kill his son.

But the angel of the LORD stopped him. The angel called from heaven and said, "Abraham, Abraham!"

Abraham answered, "Yes?"

The angel said, "Don't kill your son or hurt him in any way. Now I can see that you do respect and obey God. I see that you are ready to kill your son, your only son, for me."

Then Abraham noticed a ram whose horns were caught in a bush. So Abraham went and took the ram. He offered it, instead of his son, as a sacrifice to God. So Abraham gave that place a name, "The LORD Provides." Even today people say, "On the mountain of the LORD, he will give us what we need."

The angel of the LORD called to Abraham from heaven a second time. The angel said, "You were ready to kill your only son for me. Since you did this for me, I make you this promise: I, the LORD, promise that I will surely bless you and give you as many descendants as the stars in the sky. There will be as many people as sand on the seashore. And your people will live in cities that they will take from their enemies. Every nation on the earth will be blessed through your descendants. I will do this because you obeyed me."

STUDY TEN

Genesis 24:1-4, 10-21, 28-33, 50-54, 61-67
Here Comes the Bride

Abraham lived to be a very old man. The LORD blessed him and everything he did. Abraham's oldest servant was in charge of everything he owned. Abraham called that servant to him and said, "Put your hand under my leg. Now I want you to make a promise to me. Promise to me before the LORD, the God of heaven and earth, that you will not allow my son to marry a girl from Canaan. We live among these people, but don't let him marry a Canaanite girl. Go back to my country, to my own people, to find a wife for my son Isaac. Bring her here to him."

The servant took ten of Abraham's camels and left that place. The servant carried with him many different kinds of beautiful gifts. He went to Mesopotamia, to Nahor's city. In the evening, when the women come out to get water, he went to the water well outside the city. He made the camels kneel down at the well.

The servant said, "LORD, you are the God of my master Abraham. Please show your kindness to my master by helping me find a wife for his son Isaac. Here I am, standing by this well of water, and the young women from the city are coming out to get water. I will say to one of them, 'Please put your jar down so that I can drink.' Let her answer show whether she is the one you have chosen for your servant Isaac. If she says, 'Drink, and I will also give water to your camels,' I will know that she is the right one. It will be proof that you have shown kindness to my master."

Before the servant finished praying, a young woman named Rebekah came to the well. She was the daughter of Bethuel. (Bethuel was the son of Milcah and Nahor, Abraham's brother.) Rebekah came to the well with her water jar on her shoulder. She was very pretty. She was a virgin; no man had ever had sexual relations with her. She went down to the well and filled her jar. Then the servant ran to her and said, "Please give me a little water to drink from your jar."

Rebekah quickly lowered the jar from her shoulder and gave him a drink. She said, "Drink this, sir." As soon as she finished giving him something to drink, Rebekah said, "I will also pour some water for your camels." So Rebekah quickly poured all the water from her jar into the drinking trough for the camels. Then she ran to the well to get more water, and she gave water to all the camels.

The servant quietly watched her. He wanted to be sure that the LORD had given him an answer and had made his trip successful.

Then Rebekah ran and told her family about all these things. She had a brother named Laban. She told him what the man had said to her. Laban was listening to her. And when he saw the ring and the bracelets on his sister's arms, he ran out to the well. There the man was, standing by the camels at the well. Laban said, "Sir, you are welcome to come in! You don't have to stand outside here. I have prepared a room for you to sleep in and a place for your camels."

So Abraham's servant went into the house. Laban unloaded his camels and gave them straw and feed. Then he gave Abraham's servant water so that he and the men with him could wash their feet. Laban then gave him food to eat, but the servant refused to eat. He said, "I will not eat until I have told you why I came."

So Laban said, "Then tell us."

Then Laban and Bethuel answered, "We see that this is from the LORD, so there is nothing we can say to change it. Here is Rebekah. Take her and go. Let her marry your master's son. This is what the LORD wants."

When Abraham's servant heard this, he bowed to the ground before the LORD. Then he gave Rebekah the gifts he brought. He gave her beautiful clothes and gold and silver jewelry. He also gave expensive gifts to her mother and brother. Then he and his men had something to eat and drink, and they spent the night there. Early the next morning they got up and the servant said, "Now we must go back to my master."

Then Rebekah and her nurse got on the camels and followed the servant and his men. So the servant took Rebekah and left.

Isaac had left Beer Lahai Roi and was now living in the Negev. One evening he went out to the field to think. He looked up and saw the camels coming from far away.

Rebekah also looked and saw Isaac. Then she jumped down from the camel. She said to the servant, "Who is that young man walking in the field to meet us?"

The servant said, "That is my master's son." So Rebekah covered her face with her veil.

The servant told Isaac everything that had happened. Then Isaac brought the girl into his mother's tent. Rebekah became his wife that day. Isaac loved her very much. So he was comforted after his mother's death.

STUDY ELEVEN

Genesis 25:5-11, 19-34
It's Twins!

Before Abraham died, he gave some gifts to his sons who were from his slave women. He sent them to the East, away from Isaac. Then Abraham gave everything he owned to Isaac.

Abraham lived to be 175 years old. Then he grew weak and died. He had lived a long and satisfying life. He died and went to be with his people. His sons Isaac and Ishmael buried him in the cave of Machpelah. This cave is in the field of Ephron, the son of Zohar. It was east of Mamre. This is the same cave that Abraham bought from the Hittites. He was buried there with his wife Sarah. After Abraham died, God blessed Isaac. Isaac was living at Beer Lahai Roi.

This is the story of Isaac. Abraham had

a son named Isaac. When Isaac was 40 years old, he married Rebekah. Rebekah was from Paddan Aram. She was Bethuel's daughter and the sister of Laban the Aramean. Isaac's wife could not have children. So Isaac prayed to the LORD for her. The LORD heard Isaac's prayer, and he allowed Rebekah to become pregnant.

While Rebekah was pregnant, the babies inside her struggled with one another. She prayed to the LORD and said, "What is happening to me?" The LORD said to her,

> "The leaders of two nations are in your body.
> Two nations will come from you, and they will be divided.
> One of them will be stronger, and the older will serve the younger."

When the right time came, Rebekah gave birth to twins. The first baby was red. His skin was like a hairy robe. So he was named Esau. When the second baby was born, he was holding tightly to Esau's heel. So that baby was named Jacob. Isaac was 60 years old when Jacob and Esau were born.

The boys grew up. Esau became a skilled hunter, who loved to be out in the fields. But Jacob was a quiet man, who stayed at home. Isaac loved Esau. He liked to eat the animals Esau killed. But Rebekah loved Jacob.

One day Esau came back from hunting. He was tired and weak from hunger. Jacob was boiling a pot of beans. So Esau said to Jacob, "I am weak with hunger. Let me have some of that red soup." (That is why people call him "Red.")

But Jacob said, "You must sell me your rights as the firstborn son."

Esau said, "I am almost dead with hunger, so what good are these rights to me now?"

But Jacob said, "First, promise me that you will give them to me." So Esau made an oath to him and sold his rights as the firstborn son to Jacob. Then Jacob gave Esau bread and lentil soup. Esau ate the food, had something to drink, and then left. So Esau showed that he did not care about his rights as the firstborn son.

STUDY TWELVE

Genesis 27:1-41
Deceived!

Isaac grew old, and his eyes became so weak that he could not see clearly. One day he called his older son Esau to him and said, "Son!"

Esau answered, "Here I am."

Isaac said, "I am old. Maybe I will die soon. So take your bow and arrows and go hunting. Kill an animal for me to eat. Prepare the food that I love. Bring it to me, and I will eat it. Then I will bless you before I die." So Esau went hunting.

Rebekah was listening when Isaac told this to his son Esau. Rebekah said to her son Jacob, "Listen, I heard your father talking to your brother Esau. Your father said, 'Kill an animal for me to eat. Prepare the food for me, and I will eat it. Then, with the LORD as witness, I will bless you before I die.' So listen, son, and do what I tell you. Go out to our goats and bring me two young ones. I will prepare them the way your father loves them. Then you will carry the food to your father, and he will bless you before he dies."

But Jacob told his mother Rebekah, "My brother Esau is a hairy man. I am not hairy like him. If my father touches me, he will know that I am not Esau. Then he will not bless me—he will curse me because I tried to trick him."

So Rebekah said to him, "I will accept the blame if there is trouble. Do what I said. Go get the goats for me."

So Jacob went out and got two goats and brought them to his mother. His mother cooked the goats in the special way that Isaac loved. Then Rebekah took the clothes that her older son Esau loved to wear. She put these clothes on the younger son Jacob. She took the skins of the goats and put them on Jacob's hands and on his neck. Then she got the food she had cooked and gave it to Jacob.

Jacob went to his father and said, "Father."

His father answered, "Yes, son. Who are you?"

Jacob said to his father, "I am Esau, your first son. I have done what you told me. Now sit up and eat the meat from the animals that I hunted for you. Then you can bless me."

But Isaac said to his son, "How have you hunted and killed the animals so quickly?"

Jacob answered, "Because the LORD your God allowed me to find the animals quickly."

Then Isaac said to Jacob, "Come near to me so that I can feel you, my son. If I can feel you, I will know if you are really my son Esau."

So Jacob went to Isaac his father. Isaac felt him and said, "Your voice sounds like Jacob's voice, but your arms are hairy like the arms of Esau." Isaac did not know it was Jacob, because his arms were hairy like Esau's. So Isaac blessed Jacob.

Isaac said, "Are you really my son Esau?"

Jacob answered, "Yes, I am."

Then Isaac said, "Bring me the food. I will eat it and bless you." So Jacob gave him the food, and he ate it. Then Jacob gave him some wine, and he drank it.

Then Isaac said to him. "Son, come near and kiss me." So Jacob went to his father and kissed him. When Isaac smelled Esau's clothes, he blessed him and said,

> "My son smells like the fields
>   the LORD has blessed.
> May God give you plenty of rain,
>   good crops, and wine.
> May the nations serve you
>   and many people bow down to you.
> You will rule over your brothers.
>   Your mother's sons will bow down to you and obey you.
> Whoever curses you will be cursed.
>   Whoever blesses you will be blessed."

Isaac finished blessing Jacob. Then, just as Jacob left his father Isaac, Esau came in from hunting. Esau prepared the food in the special way his father loved. He brought it to his father and said, "Father, I am your son. Get up and eat the meat from the animals that I killed for you. Then you can bless me."

But Isaac said to him, "Who are you?"

He answered, "I am your son—your first son—Esau."

Then Isaac became so upset that he began to shake. He said, "Then who was it that cooked and brought me food before you came? I ate it all, and I blessed him. Now it is too late to take back my blessing."

When Esau heard his father's words, he became very angry and bitter. He cried out and said to his father, "Then bless me also, father!"

Isaac said, "Your brother tricked me! He came and took your blessing!"

Esau said, "His name is Jacob. That is the right name for him. He has tricked me twice. He took away my rights as the first-born son. And now he has taken away my blessing." Then Esau said, "Have you saved any blessing for me?"

Isaac answered, "I have already given Jacob the power to rule over you. And I said all his brothers would be his servants. I have given him the blessing for much grain and wine. There is nothing left to give you, my son."

But Esau continued to beg his father. "Do you have only one blessing, father? Bless me also, father!" Esau began to cry. Then Isaac said to him,

> "You will not live on good land.
>   You will not have much rain.
> You will have to fight to live,
>   and you will be a slave to your brother.
> But when you fight to be free,
>   you will break away from his control."

After that Esau hated Jacob because of this blessing. Esau said to himself, "My father will soon die, and after we are finished with that, I will kill Jacob."

STUDY THIRTEEN

Genesis 28:10-22; 29:14b-30

A Fresh Start

Jacob left Beersheba and went to Haran. The sun had already set when he came to a good place to spend the night. He took a rock there and laid his head on it to sleep. Jacob had a dream. He dreamed there was a ladder that was on the ground and reached up into heaven. He saw the angels of God going up and down the ladder. And then Jacob saw the LORD standing by the ladder. He said, "I am the LORD, the God of your grandfather Abraham. I am the God of Isaac. I will give you the land that you are lying on now. I will give this land to you and to your children. You will have as many descendants as there are particles of dust on the earth. They will spread east and west, north and south. All the families on earth will be blessed because of you and your descendants.

"I am with you, and I will protect you everywhere you go. I will bring you back to this land. I will not leave you until I have done what I have promised."

Then Jacob woke up and said, "I know that the LORD is in this place, but I did not know he was here until I slept."

Jacob was afraid and said, "This is a very great place. This is the house of God. This is the gate to heaven."

Jacob got up very early in the morning. He took the rock he had slept on and set it up on its edge. Then he poured oil on the rock. In this way he made it a memorial to God. The name of that place was Luz, but Jacob named it Bethel.

Then Jacob made a promise. He said, "If God will be with me, and if he will protect me on this trip, and if he gives me food to eat and clothes to wear, and if I return in peace to my father's house—if he does all these things—then the LORD will be my God. I am setting this stone up as a memorial stone. It will show that this is a holy place for God, and I will give God one-tenth of all he gives me."

So Jacob stayed with Laban for a month.

One day Laban said to Jacob, "You are a relative of mine. It is not right for you to continue working for me without pay. What should I pay you?"

Now Laban had two daughters. The older was Leah and the younger was Rachel.

Leah's eyes were gentle, but Rachel was beautiful. Jacob loved Rachel, so he said to Laban, "I will work seven years for you if you will allow me to marry your daughter Rachel."

Laban said, "It would be better for her to marry you than someone else. So stay with me."

So Jacob stayed and worked for Laban for seven years. But it seemed like a very short time because he loved Rachel very much.

After seven years Jacob said to Laban, "Give me Rachel so that I can marry her. My time of work for you is finished."

So Laban gave a party for all the people in that place. That night Laban brought his daughter Leah to Jacob. Jacob and Leah had sexual relations together. (Laban gave his maid Zilpah to his daughter to be her maid.) In the morning Jacob saw that it was Leah he had slept with, and he said to Laban, "You have tricked me. I worked hard for you so that I could marry Rachel. Why did you trick me?"

Laban said, "In our country we don't allow the younger daughter to marry before the older daughter. Continue for the full week of the marriage ceremony, and I will also give you Rachel to marry. But you must serve me another seven years."

So Jacob did this and finished the week. Then Laban gave him his daughter Rachel as a wife. (Laban gave his maid Bilhah to his daughter Rachel to be her maid.) So Jacob had sexual relations with Rachel also. And Jacob loved Rachel more than Leah. Jacob worked for Laban for another seven years.

STUDY FOURTEEN

Genesis 37:1-36
Danger and the Dreamer

Jacob stayed and lived in the land of Canaan. This is the same land where his father had lived. This is the story of Jacob's family.

Joseph was a young man, 17 years old. His job was to take care of the sheep and the goats. Joseph did this work with his brothers, the sons of Bilhah and Zilpah. (Bilhah and Zilpah were his father's wives.) Joseph told his father about the bad things that his brothers did. Joseph was born at a time when his father Israel was very old, so Israel loved him more than he loved his other sons. Jacob gave him a special coat, which was long and very beautiful. When Joseph's brothers saw that their father loved Joseph more than he loved them, they hated their brother because of this. They refused to say nice things to him.

One time Joseph had a special dream. Later, he told his brothers about this dream, and after that his brothers hated him even more.

Joseph said, "I had a dream. We were all working in the field, tying stacks of wheat together. Then my stack got up. It stood there while all of your stacks of wheat made a circle around mine and bowed down to it."

His brothers said, "Do you think this means that you will be a king and rule over us?" His brothers hated Joseph more now because of the dreams he had about them. Then Joseph had another dream, and he told his brothers about it. He said, "I had another dream. I saw the sun, the moon, and eleven stars bowing down to me."

Joseph also told his father about this dream, but his father criticized him. His father said, "What kind of dream is this? Do you believe that your mother, your brothers, and I will bow down to you?" Joseph's brothers continued to be jealous of him, but his father thought about all these things and wondered what they could mean.

One day Joseph's brothers went to Shechem to care for their father's sheep. Jacob said to Joseph, "Go to Shechem. Your brothers are there with my sheep."

Joseph answered, "I will go."

His father said, "Go and see if your brothers are safe. Come back and tell me if my sheep are all fine." So Joseph's father sent him from the Valley of Hebron to Shechem.

At Shechem, Joseph got lost. A man found him wandering in the fields. The man said, "What are you looking for?"

Joseph answered, "I am looking for my brothers. Can you tell me where they are with their sheep?"

The man said, "They have already gone away. I heard them say that they were going to Dothan." So Joseph followed his brothers and found them in Dothan.

Joseph's brothers saw him coming from far away. They decided to make a plan to kill him. They said to each other, "Here comes Joseph the dreamer. We should kill him now while we can. We could throw his body into one of the empty wells and tell our father that a wild animal killed him. Then we will show him that his dreams are useless."

But Reuben wanted to save Joseph. He said, "Let's not kill him. We can put him into a well without hurting him." Reuben planned to save Joseph and send him back to his father. When Joseph came to his brothers, they attacked him and tore off his long and beautiful coat. Then they threw him into an empty well that was dry.

While Joseph was in the well, the brothers sat down to eat. They looked up and saw a group of traders traveling from Gilead to Egypt. Their camels were carrying many different spices and riches. So Judah said to his brothers, "What profit will we get if we kill our brother and hide his death? We will profit more if we sell him to these traders. Then we will not be guilty of killing our own brother." The other brothers agreed. When the Midianite traders came by, the brothers took Joseph out of the well and sold him to the traders for 20 pieces of silver. The traders took him to Egypt.

Reuben had been gone, but when he came back to the well, he saw that Joseph was not there. He tore his clothes to show that he was upset. Reuben went to the brothers and said, "The boy is not in the well! What will I do?" The brothers killed a goat and put the goat's blood on Joseph's beautiful coat. Then the brothers showed the coat to their father. And the brothers said, "We found this coat. Is this Joseph's coat?"

His father saw the coat and knew that it was Joseph's. He said, "Yes, that is his! Maybe some wild animal has killed him. My son Joseph has been eaten by a wild animal!" Jacob was so sorry about his son that he tore his clothes. Then Jacob put on special clothes to show that he was sad. He continued to be sad about his son for a long time. All of Jacob's sons and daughters tried to comfort him, but Jacob was never comforted. He said, "I will be sad about my son until the day I die." So Jacob continued to mourn his son Joseph.

The Midianite traders later sold Joseph in Egypt. They sold him to Potiphar, an officer of the king of Egypt and the captain of his palace guards.

STUDY FIFTEEN

Genesis 40:1-23
Faithful and Not Forgotten

Later, two of Pharaoh's servants did something wrong to Pharaoh. These servants were the baker and the man who served wine to Pharaoh. Pharaoh became angry with his baker and wine server, so he put them in the same prison as Joseph. Potiphar, the commander of Pharaoh's guards, was in charge of this prison. The commander put the two prisoners under

Joseph's care. The two men continued to stay in prison for some time. One night both of the prisoners had a dream. The baker and the wine server each had his own dream, and each dream had its own meaning. Joseph went to them the next morning and saw that the two men were worried. He asked them, "Why do you look so worried today?"

The two men answered, "We both had dreams last night, but we don't understand what we dreamed. There is no one to explain the dreams to us."

Joseph said to them, "God is the only one who can understand and explain dreams. So I beg you, tell me your dreams."

So the wine server told Joseph his dream. The server said, "I dreamed I saw a vine. On the vine there were three branches. I watched the branches grow flowers and then become grapes. I was holding Pharaoh's cup, so I took the grapes and squeezed the juice into the cup. Then I gave the cup to Pharaoh."

Then Joseph said, "I will explain the dream to you. The three branches mean three days. Before the end of three days, Pharaoh will forgive you and allow you to go back to your work. You will do the same work for Pharaoh as you did before. But when you are free, remember me. Be good to me and help me. Tell Pharaoh about me so that I can get out of this prison. I was kidnapped and taken from the land of my people, the Hebrews. I have done nothing wrong! I should not be in prison."

The baker saw that the other servant's dream was good, so he said to Joseph, "I also had a dream. I dreamed there were three baskets of bread on my head. In the top basket there were all kinds of baked food for the king, but birds were eating this food."

Joseph answered, "I will tell you what the dream means. The three baskets mean three days. Before the end of three days, the king will take you out of this prison and cut off your head! He will hang your body on a pole, and the birds will eat it."

Three days later it was Pharaoh's birthday. He gave a party for all his servants. At the party Pharaoh allowed the wine server and the baker to leave the prison. He freed the wine server and gave him his job back, and once again the wine server put a cup of wine in Pharaoh's hand. But Pharaoh hanged the baker, and everything happened the way Joseph said it would. But the wine server did not remember to help Joseph. He said nothing about him to Pharaoh. The wine server forgot about Joseph.

STUDY SIXTEEN

Genesis 41:1-57
Promoted!

Two years later Pharaoh dreamed that he was standing by the Nile River. In the dream, seven cows came out of the river and stood there eating grass. They were healthy, good-looking cows. Then seven more cows came out of the river and stood on the bank of the river by the healthy cows. But these cows were thin and looked sick. The seven sick cows ate the seven healthy cows. Then Pharaoh woke up.

Pharaoh went back to sleep and began dreaming again. This time he dreamed that he saw seven heads of grain growing on one plant. They were healthy and full of grain. Then he saw seven more heads of grain sprouting, but they were thin and scorched by the hot wind. The thin heads of grain ate the seven good heads of grain. Then Pharaoh woke up again and realized it was only a dream. The next morning Pharaoh was worried about these dreams, so he sent for all the magicians and wise men of Egypt. Pharaoh told these men the dreams, but none of them could explain the dreams.

Then the wine servant remembered Joseph and said to Pharaoh, "I remember something that happened to me. You were angry with the baker and me, and you put us in prison. Then one night he and I had a dream. Each dream had a different meaning. There was a young Hebrew man in prison with us. He was a servant of the commander of the guards. We told him our dreams, and he explained them to us. He told us the meaning of each dream, and what he said came true. He said I would be free and have my old job back, and it happened. He also said the baker would die, and it happened!"

So Pharaoh called Joseph from the prison. The guards quickly got Joseph out of prison. Joseph shaved, put on some clean clothes, and went to see Pharaoh. Pharaoh said to Joseph, "I had a dream, and no one can explain it for me. I heard that you can explain dreams when someone tells you about them."

Joseph answered, "I cannot! But God can explain the dream for you, Pharaoh."

Then Pharaoh said to Joseph, "In my dream I was standing by the Nile River. Seven cows came up out of the river and stood there eating the grass. They were healthy, good-looking cows. Then I saw seven more cows come up out of the river after them, but these cows were thin and looked sick. They were the worst cows I had ever seen anywhere in Egypt! The thin, sick cows ate the first healthy cows, but they still looked thin and sick. You couldn't even tell they had eaten the healthy cows. They looked as thin and sick as they did in the beginning. Then I woke up.

"In my next dream I saw seven heads of grain growing on one plant. They were healthy and full of grain. And then seven more heads of grain grew after them, but they were thin and scorched by the hot wind. Then the thin heads of grain ate the seven good heads of grain.

"I told these dreams to my magicians. But no one could explain the dreams to me. What do they mean?"

Then Joseph said to Pharaoh, "Both of these dreams have the same meaning. God is telling you what will happen soon. The seven good cows and the seven good heads of grain are seven good years. And the seven thin, sick-looking cows and the seven thin heads of grain mean that there will be seven years of hunger in this area. These seven bad years will come after the seven good years. God has shown you what will happen soon. He will make these things happen just as I told you. For seven years there will be plenty of food in Egypt. But then there will be seven years of hunger. The people will forget how much food there had been in Egypt before. This famine will ruin the country. It will be so bad that people will forget what it was like to have plenty of food.

"Pharaoh, you had two dreams about the same thing. That means God wanted to show you that he really will make this happen, and he will make it happen soon! So, Pharaoh, you should choose a wise, intelligent man and put him in charge of Egypt. Then you should choose other men to collect food from the people. During the seven good years, the people must give them one-fifth of all the food they grow. In this way these men will collect all the food during the seven good years and store it in the cities until it is needed. Pharaoh, this food will be under your control. Then during the seven years of hunger, there will be food for the country of Egypt. And Egypt will not be destroyed by the famine."

This seemed like a very good idea to Pharaoh, and all his officials agreed. Then Pharaoh told them, "I don't think we can find anyone better than Joseph to take this job! God's Spirit is in him, making him very wise!"

So Pharaoh said to Joseph, "God showed these things to you, so you must be the wisest man. I will put you in charge of my country, and the people will obey all your commands. I will be the only one more powerful than you."

Pharaoh said to Joseph, "I now make you governor over all of Egypt." Then Pharaoh gave his special ring to Joseph. The royal seal was on this ring. Pharaoh also gave Joseph a fine linen robe and put a gold chain around his neck. Then he told Joseph to ride in his second chariot. Pharaoh's officials said, "Let him be the governor over the whole land of Egypt!"

Then Pharaoh said to him, "I am Pharaoh, the king over everyone in Egypt, but no one else in Egypt can lift a hand or move a foot unless you say he can." Then Pharaoh gave Joseph another name, Zaphenath Paneah. He also gave Joseph a wife named Asenath. She was the daughter of Potiphera, a priest in the city of On. So Joseph became the governor over the whole country of Egypt.

Joseph was 30 years old when he began serving the king of Egypt. He traveled throughout the country of Egypt. During the seven good years, the crops in Egypt grew very well. Joseph saved the food in Egypt during those seven years and stored the food in the cities. In every city he stored grain that grew in the fields around the city. Joseph stored so much grain that it was like the sands of the sea. He stored so much grain that it could not be measured.

Joseph's wife, Asenath, was the daughter of Potiphera, the priest in the city of

On. Before the first year of hunger came, Joseph and Asenath had two sons. Joseph named the first son Manasseh. He was given this name because Joseph said, "God made me forget all my hard work and everything back home in my father's house." Joseph named the second son Ephraim. Joseph gave him this name because he said, "I had great troubles, but God has made me successful in everything."

For seven years people had all the food they needed, but those years ended. Then the seven years of hunger began, just as Joseph had said. No food grew anywhere in any of the countries in that area. But in Egypt people had plenty to eat because Joseph had stored the grain. The famine began, and the people cried to Pharaoh for food. Pharaoh said to the Egyptian people, "Go ask Joseph what to do."

There was famine everywhere, so Joseph gave the people grain from the warehouses. He sold the stored grain to the people of Egypt. The famine was bad in Egypt, but the famine was bad everywhere. So people from the countries around Egypt had to come to Joseph in Egypt to buy grain.

STUDY SEVENTEEN

Genesis 42:1-38
Are you Spies?

During the famine in Canaan, Jacob learned that there was grain in Egypt. So he said to his sons, "Why are you sitting here doing nothing? I have heard that there is grain for sale in Egypt. Go there and buy grain for us so that we will live and not die!"

So ten of Joseph's brothers went to Egypt to buy grain. Jacob did not send Benjamin. (Benjamin was Joseph's only full brother.) Jacob was afraid that something bad might happen to Benjamin.

The famine was very bad in Canaan, so there were many people from Canaan who went to Egypt to buy grain. Among them were the sons of Israel.

Joseph was the governor of Egypt at the time. He was the one who checked the sale of grain to people who came to Egypt to buy it. Joseph's brothers came to him and bowed before him. Joseph saw his brothers and recognized them, but he acted like he didn't know them. He was rude when he spoke to them. He said, "Where do you come from?"

The brothers answered, "We have come from the land of Canaan to buy food."

Joseph recognized his brothers, but they did not know who he was. Then Joseph remembered the dreams that he had dreamed about his brothers.

Joseph said to his brothers, "You have not come to buy food! You are spies. You came to learn where we are weak."

But the brothers said to him, "No, sir, we come as your servants. We have come only to buy food. We are all brothers—we all have the same father. We are honest men. We have come only to buy food."

Then Joseph said to them, "No, you

have come to spy on us!"

And the brothers said, "No, sir, we come as servants from Canaan. We are all brothers, sons of the same father. There were twelve brothers in our family. Our youngest brother is still at home with our father, and the other brother died a long time ago."

But Joseph said to them, "No! I can see that I am right. You are spies. But I will let you prove that you are telling the truth. In the name of Pharaoh, I swear that I will not let you go until your youngest brother comes here. One of you must go back to get your youngest brother while the rest of you stay here in prison. Then we can prove whether you are telling the truth or not. If you are not telling the truth, then by Pharaoh, I swear that you are spies!" Then Joseph put them all in prison for three days.

After three days Joseph said to them, "I am a God-fearing man. Do this, and I will let you live. If you are honest men, one of your brothers can stay here in prison, and the others can go and carry grain back to your people. But then you must bring your youngest brother back here to me. Then I will know that you are telling the truth, and you will not have to die."

The brothers agreed to this. They said to each other, "We are being punished for the bad thing we did to our younger brother Joseph. We saw the trouble he was in. He begged us to save him, but we refused to listen. So now we are in trouble."

Then Reuben said to them, "I told you not to do anything bad to that boy, but you refused to listen to me. Now we are being punished for his death."

Joseph was using an interpreter to talk to his brothers, so the brothers did not know that he understood their language. He heard and understood everything they said, and that made him want to cry. So he turned away and left the room. When he came back, he took one of the brothers, Simeon, and tied him up while the others watched. Joseph told the servants to fill the bags with grain. The brothers had given Joseph the money for the grain, but he didn't keep the money. He put the money in their bags of grain. Then he gave them what they would need for their trip back home.

So the brothers put the grain on their donkeys and left. That night the brothers stopped at a place to spend the night. One of the brothers opened his sack to get some grain for his donkey. And there in the sack, he saw his money! He said to the other brothers, "Look! Here is the money I paid for the grain. Someone put the money back in my sack." The brothers were very afraid. They said to one another, "What is God doing to us?"

The brothers went back to their father Jacob in the land of Canaan. They told him about everything that had happened. They said, "The governor of that country spoke rudely to us. He thought that we were spies! We told him, 'We are honest men, not spies. There are twelve of us brothers, all from the same father. But one of our brothers is no longer living, and the youngest is still at home with our father in Canaan.'

"Then the governor of that country said to us, 'Here is a way to prove that you are honest men: Leave one of your brothers here with me. Take your grain back to your families. Bring your youngest brother to me. Then I will know if you are honest men or if you were sent from an army to destroy us. If you are telling the truth, I will give your brother back to you. I will give him to you, and you will be free to buy grain in our country.'"

Then the brothers started taking the grain out of their sacks, and every brother found his bag of money in his sack of grain. When the brothers and their father saw the money, they were afraid.

Jacob said to them, "Do you want me to lose all of my children? Joseph is gone. Simeon is gone, and now you want to take Benjamin away too!"

But Reuben said to his father, "Father, you may kill my two sons if I don't bring Benjamin back to you. Trust me. I will bring him back to you."

But Jacob said, "I will not let Benjamin go with you. His brother is dead, and he is the only son left from my wife Rachel. It would kill me if anything happened to him during the trip to Egypt. You would send me to the grave a very sad, old man."

STUDY EIGHTEEN

Genesis 43:1-15, 23b-32; 44:1-18, 33-34
Face to Face

The famine was very bad in that country. The people ate all the grain they had brought from Egypt. When that grain was gone, Jacob said to his sons, "Go to Egypt and buy some more grain for us to eat."

But Judah said to Jacob, "But the governor of that country warned us. He said, 'If you don't bring your brother back to me, I will refuse to talk to you.' If you send Benjamin with us, we will go down and buy grain. But if you refuse to send Benjamin, we will not go. The man warned us to not come back without him."

Israel said, "Why did you tell him you had another brother? Why did you do such a bad thing to me?"

The brothers answered, "He asked lots of questions. He wanted to know all about us and about our family. He asked us, 'Is your father still alive? Do you have another brother at home?' We only answered his questions. We didn't know he would ask us to bring our brother to him!"

Then Judah said to his father Israel, "Let Benjamin go with me. I will take care of him. We have to go to Egypt to get food. If we don't go, we will all die—including our children. I will make sure he is safe. I will be responsible for him. If I don't bring him back to you, you can blame me forever. If you had let us go before, we could have already made two trips for food."

Then their father Israel said, "If it is really true, take Benjamin with you. But take some gifts to the governor. Take some of the things we have been able to gather in our land. Take him some honey, pistachio nuts, almonds, spices, and myrrh. Take twice as much money with you this time. Take the money that was given back to you after you paid last time. Maybe the governor made a mistake. Take Benjamin, and go back to the man. I pray that God All-Powerful will help you when you stand before the governor. I pray that he will let Benjamin, and also Simeon, come back safely. If not, I will again be sad from losing my children."

So the brothers took the gifts to give to the governor. And the brothers took twice as much money with them as they took the first time. This time Benjamin went with the brothers to Egypt.

But the servant answered, "Don't be afraid; believe me. Your God, the God of your father, must have put the money in your sack as a gift. I remember that you paid me for the grain the last time."

Then the servant brought Simeon out of the prison. The servant led the men into Joseph's house. He gave them water, and they washed their feet. Then he fed their donkeys.

The brothers heard that they were going to eat with Joseph, so they worked until noon preparing their gifts for him.

When Joseph came home, the brothers gave him the gifts they had brought with them. Then they bowed down to the ground in front of him.

Joseph asked them how they were doing. Then he said, "How is your elderly father you told me about? Is he still alive?"

The brothers answered, "Yes, sir, our father is still alive." And they again bowed before Joseph.

Then Joseph saw his brother Benjamin. (Benjamin and Joseph had the same mother.) Joseph said, "Is this your youngest brother that you told me about?" Then Joseph said to Benjamin, "God bless you, my son!"

Joseph felt a strong desire to show his brother Benjamin that he loved him. He was about to cry and didn't want his brothers to see him, so he ran into his private room and cried there. Then Joseph washed his face and came out. He regained control of himself and said, "Now it is time to eat."

The servants seated Joseph at a table by himself. His brothers were at another table by themselves, and the Egyptians were at a table by themselves. The Egyptians believed that it was wrong for them to eat with Hebrews.

Then Joseph gave a command to his servant. He said, "Fill the men's sacks with as much grain as they can carry. Then put each man's money into his sack with the grain. Put the youngest brother's money in his sack too. But also put my special silver cup in his sack." So the servant obeyed Joseph.

Early the next morning the brothers and their donkeys were sent back to their country. After they had left the city, Joseph said to his servant, "Go and follow the men. Stop them and say to them, 'We were good to you! So why have you been bad to us? Why did you steal my master's silver cup? My master drinks from that cup, and he uses it to learn secret things. What you did was wrong!'"

So the servant obeyed. He rode out to the brothers and stopped them. The servant said to them what Joseph had told him to say.

But the brothers said to the servant, "Why does the governor say these things? We wouldn't do anything like that! We brought back the money that we found in our sacks before. So surely we wouldn't steal silver or gold from your master's house. If you find the silver cup in any of our sacks, let that man die. You can kill him, and we will be your slaves."

The servant said, "I agree, except that only the man who is found to have the cup will be my slave. The others will be free."

Then every brother quickly opened his sack on the ground. The servant started looking in the sacks. He started with the oldest brother and ended with the youngest. He found the cup in Benjamin's sack. The brothers were very sad. They tore their clothes to show their sadness. They put their sacks back on the donkeys and went back to the city.

When Judah and his brothers went back to Joseph's house, Joseph was still there. The brothers fell to the ground and bowed down before him. Joseph said to them, "Why have you done this? Didn't you know that I have a special way of learning secrets? No one is better at this than I am!"

Judah said, "Sir, there is nothing we can say. There is no way to explain. There is no way to show that we are not guilty. God has judged us guilty for something else we have done. So all of us, even Benjamin, will be your slaves."

But Joseph said, "I will not make you all slaves! Only the man who stole the cup will be my slave. You others can go in peace to your father."

Then Judah went to Joseph and said, "Sir, please let me speak plainly with you. Please don't be angry with me. I know that you are like Pharaoh himself. So now I beg you, please let the boy go back with his brothers, and I will stay and be your slave. I cannot go back to my father if the boy is not with me. I am very afraid of what would happen to my father."

STUDY NINETEEN

Genesis 45:1—46:7
I Am Joseph

Joseph could not control himself any longer. He cried in front of all the people who were there. Joseph said, "Tell everyone to leave here." So all the people left. Only the brothers were left with Joseph. Then he told them who he was. Joseph continued to cry, and all the Egyptian people in Pharaoh's house heard it. He said to his brothers, "I am your brother Joseph. Is my father doing well?" But the brothers did not answer him because they were confused and afraid.

So Joseph said to his brothers again, "Come here to me. I beg you, come here." When the brothers went to him, he said to them, "I am your brother Joseph. I am the one you sold as a slave to Egypt. Now don't be worried. Don't be angry with yourselves for what you did. It was God's plan for me to come here. I am here to save people's lives. This terrible famine has continued for two years now, and there will be five more years without planting or harvest. So God sent me here ahead of you so that I can save your people in this country. It was not your fault that I was sent here. It was God's plan. God made me like a father to Pharaoh. I am the governor over all his house and over all Egypt."

Joseph said, "Hurry up and go to my father. Tell him his son Joseph sent this message: 'God made me the governor of Egypt. So come here to me quickly. Don't wait. You can live near me in the land of Goshen. You, your children, your grandchildren, and all of your animals are welcome here. I will take care of you during the next five years of hunger. So you and your family will not lose everything you own.'

"Surely you can see that I really am Joseph. Even my brother Benjamin knows it is me, your brother, talking to you. So tell my father about the honor I have received here in Egypt. Tell him about everything you have seen here. Now hurry, go bring my father back to me." Then Joseph hugged his brother Benjamin, and they both began crying. Then Joseph cried as he kissed all his brothers. After this, the brothers began talking with him.

Pharaoh learned that Joseph's brothers had come to him. This news spread throughout Pharaoh's house. Pharaoh and his servants were very excited! So Pharaoh told Joseph, "Tell your brothers to take all the food they need and go back to the land of Canaan. Tell them to bring your father and their families back here to me. I will give you the best land in Egypt to live on. And your family can eat the best food we have here. Also give your brothers some of our best wagons. Tell them to go to Canaan and bring your father and all the women and children back in the wagons. Don't worry about bringing all of their belongings. We can give them the best of Egypt." So the sons of Israel did this. Joseph gave them good wagons just as Pharaoh had promised. And Joseph gave them enough food for their trip. He gave each brother a suit of beautiful clothes. But to Benjamin he gave five suits of beautiful clothes and 300 pieces of silver. Joseph also sent gifts to his father. He sent ten donkeys with bags full of many good things from Egypt. And he sent ten female donkeys loaded with grain, bread, and other food for his father on his trip back. Then Joseph told his brothers to go. While they were leaving, he said to them, "Go straight home, and don't fight on the way."

So the brothers left Egypt and went to their father in the land of Canaan. They told him, "Father, Joseph is still alive! And he is the governor over the whole country of Egypt."

Their father did not know what to think. At first he didn't believe them. But then they told him everything Joseph had said. Then their father saw the wagons that Joseph had sent to bring him back to Egypt, and he became excited and very happy. Israel said, "Now I believe you. My son Joseph is still alive! I am going to see him before I die!"

So Israel began his trip to Egypt. First he went to Beersheba. There he worshiped God, the God of his father Isaac. He offered sacrifices. During the night God spoke to Israel in a dream and said, "Jacob, Jacob."

Israel answered, "Here I am."

Then God said, "I am God, the God of your father. Don't be afraid to go to Egypt. In Egypt I will make you a great nation. I will go to Egypt with you, and I will bring you out of Egypt again. You will die there, but Joseph will be with you. His own hands will close your eyes when you die."

Then Jacob left Beersheba and traveled to Egypt. His sons, the sons of Israel, brought their father, their wives, and all their children to Egypt. They traveled in the wagons the Pharaoh had sent. They also had their cattle and everything they owned in the land of Canaan. So Israel went to Egypt with all his children and his family. With him were his sons and his grandsons, his daughters and his granddaughters. All of his family went with him.

STUDY TWENTY

Genesis 46:28-32; 50:14-26
Promises Fulfilled

Jacob sent Judah ahead to speak to Joseph. Judah went to Joseph in the land of Goshen. Then Jacob and his people followed into the land. Joseph learned that his father was coming. So he prepared his chariot and went out to meet his father, Israel, in Goshen. When Joseph saw his father, he hugged his neck and cried for a long time.

Then Israel said to Joseph, "Now I can die in peace. I have seen your face, and I know that you are still alive."

Joseph said to his brothers and to the rest of his father's family, "I will go and tell Pharaoh that you are here. I will say to Pharaoh, 'My brothers and the rest of my father's family have left the land of Canaan and have come here to me. They are a family of shepherds. They have always kept sheep and cattle. They have brought all their animals and everything they own with them.'

After Joseph buried his father, he and everyone in the group with him went back to Egypt.

After Jacob died, Joseph's brothers were worried. They were afraid that Joseph would still be mad at them for what they had done years before. They said, "Maybe Joseph still hates us for what we did." So the brothers sent this message to Joseph: "Before your father died, he told us to give you a message. He said, 'Tell Joseph that I beg him to please forgive his brothers for the bad things they did to him.' So now Joseph, we beg you, please forgive us for the bad things we did to you. We are the servants of God, the God of your father."

That message made Joseph very sad, and he cried. His brothers went to him and bowed down in front of him. They said, "We will be your servants."

Then Joseph said to them, "Don't be afraid. I am not God! I have no right to punish you. It is true that you planned to do something bad to me. But really, God was planning good things. God's plan was to use me to save the lives of many people. And that is what happened. So don't be afraid. I will take care of you and your children." And so Joseph said kind things to his brothers, and this made them feel better.

Joseph continued to live in Egypt with his father's family. He died when he was 110 years old. During Joseph's life Ephraim had children and grandchildren. And his son Manasseh had a son named Makir. Joseph lived to see Makir's children.

When Joseph was near death, he said to his brothers, "My time to die is almost here. But I know that God will take care of you and lead you out of this country. God will lead you to the land he promised to give Abraham, Isaac, and Jacob."

Then Joseph asked his people to make a promise. Joseph said, "Promise me that you will carry my bones with you when God leads you out of Egypt."

Joseph died in Egypt when he was 110 years old. Doctors prepared his body for burial and put the body in a coffin in Egypt.

CHILDREN'S BIBLE QUIZZING

Children's Bible Quizzing is an optional part of *Bible Studies for Children*. Each church and each child decides whether to participate in a series of competitive events.

Quizzing events follow the rules outlined in this book. Children do not compete against each other to determine a single winner. Churches do not compete against each other to determine a winner.

The purpose of Quizzing is to help the children to determine what they learned about the Bible, to enjoy the competitive events, and to grow in the ability to display Christian attitudes and Christian behaviours during competitive events.

In Quizzing, each child challenges himself or herself to attain an award level. In this approach, children quiz against a base of knowledge, not against each other. Quizzing uses a multiple-choice approach that allows every child to answer every question. Multiple choice questions offer several answers, and the child chooses the correct one. This approach makes it possible for every child to be a winner.

QUIZZING SUPPLIES

Each child needs Quizzing numbers to answer the questions. Quizzing numbers are four cardboard squares that each have a tab at the top with the numbers 1, 2, 3, and 4 respectively. The numbers fit inside a cardboard box.

You can order cardboard Quizzing boxes and numbers, pictured here, from the Nazarene Publishing House in Kansas City, Missouri, United States of America.

If cardboard Quizzing boxes and numbers are not available in your area, you can make your own Quizzing numbers from paper, paper plates, wood, or whatever you have available. Each child needs a set of Quizzing numbers.

Each group of children will need a person to score their answers. There is a reproducible score sheet on page 155. Use this score sheet to keep track of the answers of each child.

If possible, provide some type of an award for the performance of the children in each Quizzing event. Suggested awards are certificates, stickers, ribbons, trophies, or medals. Certificate templates are included on pages 153 and 154.

Please follow these rules. Competitions that do not operate in accordance with the *Children's Quizzing Official Competition Rules and Procedures* will not qualify for other competition levels.

AGES AND GRADES

Children in grades 1-6* may participate in Children's Quizzing competitions. Seventh graders, regardless of age, participate in Teen Quizzing.

BASIC LEVEL COMPETITION

This competition level is for younger or beginning quizzers. Older quizzers who prefer an easier level of competition may also participate in the Basic Level. The questions for the Basic Level are simpler. There are three answers for each question, and there are fifteen questions in each round. The district or regional Children's Quizzing director determines the questions and the number of rounds at each Quizzing competition. Most competitions have two or three rounds.

ADVANCED LEVEL COMPETITION

This competition level is for older quizzers or experienced quizzers. Younger quizzers who want a greater challenge may participate in the Advanced Level. The questions for the Advanced Level are more compre-

hensive. There are four answers for each question, and there are twenty questions in each round. The district or regional Children's Quizzing director determines the questions and the number of rounds at each Quizzing event.

SWITCHING BETWEEN LEVELS

Children may switch between Basic Level and Advanced Level only for invitational Quizzing competitions. This helps the leaders and the children determine the best level for each child. For the zone/area, the district, and the regional competitions, the local director must register each child for either Basic Level or Advanced Level. The child must compete at the same level for zone/area, district, and regional competitions.

TYPES OF COMPETITION

Invitational Competition

An invitational competition is between two or more churches. Local Children's Quizzing directors, zone/area Children's Quizzing directors, or district Children's Quizzing directors may organize invitational competitions. Individuals who organize an invitational competition have the responsibility to prepare the competition questions.

*For countries other than the United States, grades 1-6 are generally ages 6-12.

Zone/Area Competition

Each district may have smaller groupings of churches that are called zones. If one zone has more quizzers than another zone, the district Children's Quizzing director may separate or combine the zones to create areas with a more equitable distribution of quizzers. The term area means combined or divided zones.

The churches located in each zone/area compete in that zone/area. The district Children's Quizzing director organizes the competition. Questions for the zone/area competitions are official questions.

E-mail *ChildQuiz@nazarene.org* to request these questions from the General Children's Quizzing Office.

District Competition

Children advance from the zone/area competition to the district competition. The district Children's Quizzing director determines the qualifications for the competition and organizes the competition.

Questions for district competitions are official questions. E-mail *ChildQuiz@nazarene.org* to request these questions from the General Children's Quizzing Office.

Regional Competition

The regional competition is a competition between two or more districts.

When there is a regional Children's Quizzing director, he or she determines the qualifications for the competition and organizes the competition. If there is not a regional director, the participating district directors organize the competition.

Questions for the regional competitions are official questions. To request these questions from the General Children's Quizzing Office, e-mail *ChildQuiz@nazarene.org.*

WORLD QUIZ COMPETITION

Every four years, the General Children's Quizzing Office in conjunction with Sunday School and Discipleship Ministries International sponsors an international World Quiz. The Global Children's Quizzing Office determines the dates, the locations, the costs, the qualifying dates, and the overall qualifying process for all World Quiz competitions. E-mail *ChildQuiz@nazarene.org* for more information.

DISTRICT CHILDREN'S QUIZZING DIRECTOR

The district Children's Quizzing director operates all competitions according to the *Children's Quizzing Official Competition Rules and Procedures.* He or she has the authority to introduce additional Quizzing procedures on the district as long as the procedures do not conflict with the *Children's Quizzing Official Competition Rules and Procedures.* The district Children's Quizzing director contacts the General Children's Quizzing Office, when necessary, to request a specific change in the *Children's Quizzing Official Competition Rules and Procedures* for a district. The district Children's Quizzing director makes the decisions and solves the problems within the guidelines of the *Children's Quizzing Official Competition Rules and Procedures.* The district Children's Quizzing director contacts the General Children's Quizzing Office for an official ruling on a specific situation, if necessary.

REGIONAL CHILDREN'S QUIZZING DIRECTOR

The regional Children's Quizzing director creates a regional Children's Quizzing leadership team that consists of all of the district Children's Quizzing directors on the region. The regional Children's Quizzing director remains in contact with this team to keep the procedures consistent across the region. He or she operates and organizes the regional competitions according to the *Children's Quizzing Official Competition Rules and Procedures*. The regional Children's Quizzing director contacts the General Children's Quizzing Office to request any changes in the *Children's Quizzing Official Competition Rules and Procedures* for a specific region. He or she resolves any conflicts that arise with the help of the guidelines of the *Children's Quizzing Official Competition Rules and Procedures.* The regional Children's Quizzing director contacts the General Children's Quizzing

Office for an official ruling on a specific situation, if necessary. He or she contacts the General Children's Quizzing Office to place the regional quiz date on the general church calendar. In the United States and Canada, the regional Children's Quizzing director is a developing position. Currently that person does not preside over district Children's Quizzing directors on the region.

QUIZMASTER

The quizmaster reads the competition questions at a Quizzing competition. The quizmaster reads the question and the multiple-choice answers two times before the children answer the question. He or she follows the *Children's Quizzing Official Competition Rules and Procedures* established by the General Children's Quizzing Office and the district Children's Quizzing director/regional coordinator. In the event of a conflict, the final authority is the district/regional Children's Quizzing director who consults the *Children's Quizzing Official Competition Rules and Procedures*. The quizmaster may participate in discussions with scorekeepers and the district/regional Children's Quizzing director about a challenge. The quizmaster may call a time-out.

SCOREKEEPER

The scorekeeper scores a group of children's answers. He or she may participate in discussions with scorekeepers and the district/regional Children's Quizzing director about a challenge. All scorekeepers are to use the same method and the same symbols to insure correct tabulation of the scores.

OFFICIAL COMPETITION QUESTIONS

The district Children's Quizzing director is the only individual on the district who may obtain a copy of the official zone/area and district competition questions.

The regional Children's Quizzing director is the only individual on the region who may obtain a copy of the official regional competition questions. If there is not a regional Children's Quizzing director, one participating district Children's Quizzing director may obtain a copy of the official regional competition questions.

Order forms for annual official questions will be sent by E-mail each year. Contact the General Children's Quizzing Office at *ChildQuiz@nazarene.org* to update your E-mail address. The official questions will arrive by Email to the people who request them.

COMPETITION METHODS

There are two methods of competition.

Individual method

In the individual method of competition, the children compete as individual children. The score of each child is separate from all other scores. Children from the same church may sit together, but do not add together the individual scores to obtain a church or a team score. There are no bonus questions for individual quizzers.

The individual method is the only method to use for the Basic Level competition.

Combination Method

The combination method combines individual and team Quizzing. In this method, churches may send individual quizzers, the teams, or a combination of these to a competition.

The district Children's Quizzing director determines the number of children needed to form a team. All teams must have the same number of quizzers. The recommended number for a team is four or five children.

The children from the churches that do not have enough quizzers to form a team can compete as individual quizzers.

In the combination method, teams qualify for bonus questions. The bonus points awarded for a correct answer to a bonus question become part of the total score of the team, instead of a score for an individual quizzer. There are bonus questions with the official questions for zone/area, district, and regional competitions. Bonus questions typically involve the recitation of a memory verse.

The district Children's Quizzing director selects either the individual method or the combination method for the Advanced Level of the competition.

TIE SCORES

Ties between individual quizzers or the teams remain as tied scores. All individual children or teams who tie receive the same recognition, the same award, and the same advancement to the next level of competition.

BONUS QUESTIONS

Bonus questions are part of the Advanced Level, but only with teams, not individuals. Teams must qualify for a bonus question. Bonus questions occur after questions 5, 10, 15, and 20.

To qualify for a bonus question, a team may have only as many incorrect answers as there are members on the team. For example, a team of four members may have four or fewer answers that are incorrect. A team of five members may have five or fewer answers that are incorrect.

The bonus points for a correct answer become part of the total score of the team, not of the individual score of a child.

The district Children's Quizzing director determines the way that the children answer bonus questions. In most situations, the child verbally gives the answer to the scorekeeper.

Prior to the reading of the bonus question, the local Children's Quizzing director selects one team member to answer the bonus question. The same child may answer all of the bonus questions in a game, or a different child may answer each bonus question.

TIME-OUTS

The district Children's Quizzing director determines the number of time-outs for each church. Each church receives the same number of time-outs, regardless of the number of individual quizzers or teams from that church. For example, if the district director decides to give one time-out, each church receives one timeout.

The district Children's Quizzing director determines if an automatic time-out will occur during the game and the specific point at which the time-out will occur in each game.

The local Children's Quizzing director is the only individual who may call a time-out for a local church team.

The district Children's Quizzing director or quizmaster may call a time-out at any time. The district Children's Quizzing director, prior to the start of the competition, determines the maximum length of the time-outs for the competition.

SCORING

There are two methods for scoring. The district Children's Quizzing director selects the method.
Five Points
- Award five points for every correct

answer. For example, if a child answers 20 questions correctly in an Advanced Level round, the child earns a total of 100 points.

- Award five points for every correct bonus answer in an Advanced Level team Quizzing round. For example, if every member of a team with four persons answers 20 questions correctly in an Advanced Level round and the team answers four bonus questions correctly, the team earns a total of 420 points.

Basic Level points will be lower as there are only 15 questions per round, and it is individual competition only.

One Point

Award one point for each correct answer as follows:

- Award one point for every correct answer. For example, if a child answers 20 questions correctly in an Advanced level round, the child earns a total of 20 points.
- Award one point for every correct bonus answer in an Advanced Level team Quizzing round. For example, if every member of a team with four persons answers 20 questions correctly in an Advanced Level round and the team answers four bonus questions correctly, the team earns a total of 84 points.

Basic Level points will be lower as there are only 15 questions per round, and it is individual competition only.

CHALLENGES

Challenges are to be an exception and are not common during a competition.

Request a challenge only when the answer marked as correct in the questions is actually incorrect according to the Bible reference given for that question. Challenges issued for any other reason are invalid.

A quizzer, a Children's Quizzing director, or any other competition participant may not request a challenge because they dislike the wording of a question or answer or think a question is too difficult or confusing.

The local Children's Quizzing director is the only person who may issue a challenge to a competition question.

If an individual other than the local Children's Quizzing director attempts to issue a challenge, the challenge is automatically ruled as "invalid."

Individuals who issue invalid challenges disrupt competition and cause the children to lose their concentration. Individuals who consistently issue invalid challenges or create some problems by arguing about a challenge ruling will lose their privilege of challenging the questions for the remainder of the competition.

The district Children's Quizzing director, or the quizmaster in the absence of the district Children's Quizzing director, has the authority to remove the privilege of challenging questions from any or all individuals who abuse the privilege.

The district Children's Quizzing director determines how to challenge a competition question prior to the start of the competition.

- Will the challenge be written or verbal?
- When can a person challenge (during a game or at the end of a game)?

The district Children's Quizzing director should explain the procedure for the challenges to local Children's Quizzing directors at the beginning of the quiz year.

The quizmaster and district Children's Quizzing director follow these steps to rule the challenge.

- Determine if the challenge is valid or invalid. To do this, listen to the reason for the challenge. If the reason is valid, the answer given as the correct answer is incorrect according to the Bible reference, follow the challenge procedures outlined by the district.
- If the reason for the challenge is invalid, announce that the challenge is invalid, and the competition continues.

If more than one person challenges the same question, the quizmaster or district Children's Quizzing director selects one local quiz director to explain the reason for a challenge. After a question has one challenge, another person may not challenge the same question.

If a challenge is valid, the district Children's Quizzing director, or quizmaster in the director's absence, determines how to handle the challenged question. Select one of the following options.

Option A: Eliminate the question, and do not replace it. The result is that a game of 20 questions becomes a game of 19 questions.

Option B: Give every child the points he or she would receive for a correct answer to the challenged question.

Option C: Replace the challenged question. Ask the quizzers a new question. Option D: Let the children who gave the answer that was listed as the correct answer in the official questions keep their points. Give another question to the children who gave an answer that was an incorrect answer.

AWARD LEVELS

Children's Quizzing has the philosophy that every child has an opportunity to answer every question, and every child receives recognition for every correct answer he or she gives. Therefore, Children's Quizzing uses multiple-choice competition, and ties are never broken.

Children and churches do not compete against each other. They compete to reach an award level. All of the children and all of the churches who reach the same award level receive the same award. Ties remain as tied scores.

Recommended Award Levels:
Bronze Award = 70-79% correct
Silver Award = 80-89% correct

Gold Award = 90-99% correct

Gold All Star = 100% correct

Resolve all scoring and challenge decisions before presenting awards. The quizmaster and scorekeepers should be sure that all final scores are accurate prior to the presentation.

Never take an award from a child after the child receives an award. If there is a mistake, children may receive a higher award but not a lower award. This is true for individual awards and team awards.

COMPETITION ETHICS

The district Children's Quizzing director is the person on the district who has the responsibility to conduct the competitions in accordance with the *Children's Quizzing Official Competition Rules and Procedures.*

- **Hearing Questions Before the Competition.** Since competitions use the same questions, it is not appropriate for the children and the workers to attend another zone/area, district, or regional competition prior to their participation in their own competition of the same level. If an adult Quizzing worker attends another competition, the district Children's Quizzing director may choose to disqualify the church from participation in their competition. If a parent and/or child attends another competition, the district Children's Quizzing director may choose to disqualify the church from participation in their competition.

- **Worker's Conduct and Attitudes.** Adults are to conduct themselves in a professional and in a Christian manner. The discussions about disagreements with the district Children's Quizzing director, quizmaster, or scorekeepers are to be private. Adult Quizzing workers should not share information about the disagreement with the children. A cooperative spirit and good sportsmanship are important. The decisions and the rulings of the district Children's Quizzing director are final. Relay these decisions in a positive tone to the children and to the adults.

CHEATING

Any cheating is serious. Treat the cheating seriously.

The district Children's Quizzing director, in discussion with the district Children's Ministries Council, determines the policy to follow in the event that a child or an adult cheats during a competition.

Make sure that all local children's ministries directors, children's pastors, and local Children's Quizzing directors receive the policy and the procedures of the district. Before accusing an adult or a child of cheating, have some evidence or a witness that the cheating occurred.

Ensure that the quiz continues and that

the person accused of cheating does not suffer embarrassment in front of other people. Here is a sample procedure.

- If you suspect that a child cheated, ask someone to serve as a judge to watch the areas, but do not point out any child whom you suspect. After a few questions, ask the opinion of the judge. If the judge did not see any cheating, continue with the quiz.
- If the judge saw a child who was cheating, ask the judge to affirm it. Do not act until everyone is sure. Explain the problem to the local Children's Quizzing director, and ask the director to talk with the accused person privately.
- The quizmaster, the judge, and the local Children's Quizzing director should watch for continued cheating.
- If the cheating continues, the quizmaster and the local Children's Quizzing director should talk with the accused person privately.
- If the cheating continues, the quizmaster should tell the local Children's Quizzing director that he or she will eliminate the score of the child from official competition.
- In the case that a scorekeeper cheated, the district Children's Quizzing director will ask the scorekeeper to leave, and a new scorekeeper will take his or her place.
- In the case that someone in the audience cheated, the district Children's Quizzing director will handle the situation in the most appropriate manner.

UNRESOLVED DECISIONS

Consult with the General Children's Quizzing Office regarding unresolved decisions.

CERTIFICATE OF COMPLETION

presented to

_____

NAME

Congratulations for successfully completing

Bible Studies for Children: Genesis

_____
Date

_____
Location

_____
Teacher

Award for Excellence

presented to

_____
NAME

Great job! We recognize your outstanding

achievement in *Bible Studies for Children: Genesis*

_____
Date

_____
Location

_____
Teacher

ATTENDANCE SHEET

Write the children's names in the lines provided. Place an X in the column for each lesson the child is in attendance. You may reproduce this attendance sheet if you need more lines.

Name	1	2	3	4	5	6	7	8	9	10	11	12	13	14	15	16	17	18	19	20

CHILDREN'S QUIZZING SCORE SHEET

Instructions: Basic Quizzing uses only questions 1-15. Advanced quizzing uses 20 questoins. Read the *Official Rules and Procedures* for complete instructions.

Names:

Round 1	1	2	3	4	5	6	7	8	9	10	11	12	13	14	15	16	17	18	19	20	Total

Team Bonus:

Team Total

Names:

Round 2	1	2	3	4	5	6	7	8	9	10	11	12	13	14	15	16	17	18	19	20	Total

Team Bonus:

Team Total

Names:

Round 3	1	2	3	4	5	6	7	8	9	10	11	12	13	14	15	16	17	18	19	20	Total

Team Bonus:

Team Total

THANK YOU!

Thank you to everyone who contributed to the 2008-2009 Kids Reaching Kids Mission Offering Project: The D-Code Challenge. Your gifts made the Bible Studies for Children series of six books possible: 1 & 2 Samuel; Matthew; Acts; Genesis; Exodus; and Joshua, Judges and Ruth.

Every year, children from over 1,000 local organizations from all across the globe give to this project. In addition to the money raised for Bible Studies for Children, Kids Reaching Kids impacts children all over the world in a number of amazing ways. This special offering is named well. It really is a way for kids to help kids.

Here is an update on other projects sponsored by you through Kids Reaching Kids:

Kids Reaching Kids: The Hope Project (2009-2010):

- Supplying basic needs for the children at Herstelling Compassionate Center in Guayana.
- Aiding the Haiti Hot Lunch program and Haiti Water Project.
- Caring for orphans of aids and vulnerable children in Africa.
- Bringing hope to families and to disabled children in Tonga.
- Helping children and families affected by the 8.9 magnitude earthquake in Japan.
- Helping orphans in Vidrare, Bulgaria.
- Helping inner-city children through Cincinnati Urban Promise in Ohio, USA.

Kids Reaching Kids: Mission STAR Quest:

- Supporting the effort to find solutions of poverty at the Center of Hope in South Africa.
- Educating children and families in Mozambique through the Community Health Evangelism program.
- Purchasing computers and desks for Christian schools in the Middle East.
- Enabling the children at the Nazarene school in Beirut, Lebanon to have reliable heat and electricity.
- Aiding in the efforts of the Amador Street Hope Center in Vellajo, California, USA.
- Helping to rebuild churches and schools in Haiti and the Dominican Republic affected by hurricanes.

These are just a portion of all that Kids Reaching Kids is doing for children all across the world. In 2011-2012, children are raising money through His Hands: Jesus, Miracles, Medicine and Me. Money raised through this offering will help meet the medical needs for children and their families. All proceeds are divided equally among the six Nazarene world regions. Join us as we unite in Jesus Christ to bring hope to our world.

For more information about Kids Reaching Kids, and to support His Hands and future offering efforts, contact your regional SDMI representative. *Also, visit our website at: www.kidsreachingkids.com.*